MW01487116

MURDER
in OLD FORGE
PENNSYLVANIA

MURDER
in OLD FORGE
PENNSYLVANIA

The Tragic Death of the
Ziemba Children

BRIAN W. KINCAID

THE
History
PRESS

Published by The History Press
An imprint of Arcadia Publishing
Charleston, SC
www.historypress.com

Copyright © 2025 by Brian Kincaid

Cover images from the *Scranton Times-Tribune*, via the Lackawanna County Historical Society.

All rights reserved

First published 2025

Manufactured in the United States

ISBN 9781467157155

Library of Congress Control Number: 2025935717

Notice: The information in this book is true and complete to the best of our knowledge. It is offered without guarantee on the part of the author or The History Press. The author and The History Press disclaim all liability in connection with the use of this book.

All rights reserved. No part of this book may be reproduced or transmitted in any form whatsoever without prior written permission from the publisher except in the case of brief quotations embodied in critical articles and reviews.

In memory of Cheryl Lynn Ziemba, age eight,
and Christopher Ziemba, age four,
murdered by Joey Aulisio on July 26, 1981.

CONTENTS

CONTENTS

ACKNOWLEDGEMENTS

I would firstly like to thank Old Forge firefighter Stanley Zoltewicz, without whom this true crime story never would have been written. Stanley spent countless hours with me over a period of thirty years recounting the July 1981 search efforts to find the Ziemba children, introduced me to people with knowledge of the Ziemba murder case and walked various crime scenes with me. Thanks also goes to Old Forge firefighters Mike Nalevanko, Ed Orzalek and Frank Genell, all of whom shared their thoughts with me regarding those terrible days in July 1981 when they took part in the search for the Ziemba children. The late Jack Brier indulged me for a lengthy interview and opened his file to me. The late jurist Judge James Walsh was kind enough to sit with me in his chambers for an interview. Former Lackawanna County District Attorney Ernie Preate Jr. sat for an interview with me while he was serving as Pennsylvania attorney general. During several interviews and phone calls, Major Mike Jordan (ret.) of the Pennsylvania State Police provided me with valuable insights regarding the investigation of the Ziemba murders. The late Pennsylvania State Trooper Nicky Genova had welcomed me into his home for an interview. Lackawanna County District Attorney (now Common Pleas Court Judge) Mark Powell encouraged me, following my testimony in the December 2019 hearing, to recommence working on this book after my research and book outline had remained untouched for nearly twenty years. The late Lenny Brown and the late Doreen Propersi allowed me a brief interview on the sidewalk outside their home in Old Forge. I spent a Saturday afternoon with the late Robert Aulisio Sr. in 1989, hearing a different perspective on this murder case. Many thanks to several Old Forge residents who wished to remain anonymous but who shared their knowledge and private thoughts regarding the Ziemba murders. Thank you to Robert Zigmund, a law school friend, who made me aware of the Ziemba murders case and encouraged me to write this story. Thank you to my legal assistants Michelle Oswald, Lauren Wyckoff and Dawn McOwan for their invaluable assistance in putting words to paper. Many thanks to several of my fellow firefighters of the Mount Arlington, New Jersey Fire and Rescue Company and Roxbury Fire Company 2 who indulged me and read over countless drafts of this book. Finally, thank you to my family, friends and all those who believed in this project.

INTRODUCTION

On a rainy Sunday afternoon on July 26, 1981, eight-year-old Cheryl Lynn Ziemba and her four-year-old brother, Christopher, disappeared from their backyard in Old Forge, Pennsylvania, never to be seen alive again. Police, firefighters and hundreds of volunteers searched frantically for Cheryl Lynn and Christopher for two days, only to find the children's bodies dumped like garbage in an abandoned strip mining pit. The search for the Ziemba children soon turned into an equally desperate search for their killer. It was beyond shocking to Old Forge residents when Joey Aulisio, fifteen-year-old neighbor of the Ziemba family, was arrested on July 29, 1981, and charged with the murders of Cheryl Lynn and Christopher.

National headlines were made, and international outrage occurred when in May 1982 Joey Aulisio was convicted of two counts of first-degree murder and sentenced to die in Pennsylvania's electric chair. The imposition of the death penalty by the jury made Aulisio, for a time, the youngest death row inmate in the United States. A long series of appeals followed Aulisio's incarceration. In 1987, the death sentence was reversed, but his murder convictions were upheld, meaning that he now faced life, without parole, behind bars. From July 1981 through December 2019, Joey Aulisio never admitted to any responsibility for the murders of young Cheryl Lynn and Christopher Ziemba. This changed during a December 2019 hearing for resentencing, when Aulisio sought to be released for time served thus far on his life sentence. During the hearing, Aulisio finally admitted and revealed under oath what happened to the Ziemba children on July 26, 1981.

Major crime investigations are painstaking endeavors. Criminal murder trials tend to be seen as melodramas, and the behind-the-scenes drama is usually not known to the public. Truth and facts at a criminal trial are often blurred by the arguments of defense counsel and prosecutors. Thus, while certain facts regarding a major criminal case may be known on the surface by an individual who follows current events, the actual story remains unknown. The story of the murder trial is often as remarkable as the crime being brought to trial.

The passing of time dulls memories of even a major murder case. Not so in Old Forge, Pennsylvania, as the memory of the Ziemba murder case remains sharp after the passage of forty-four years, and the remembrance of Cheryl Lynn and Christopher Ziemba continues to be sacred. This is the story of one of the most shocking murder investigations and trials in the history of the Commonwealth of Pennsylvania.

A SUMMER AFTERNOON

The drive home to Old Forge, Pennsylvania, from a visit to New York City on Saturday, July 25, 1981, for Diane Ziemba and her sister, Linda Jo, was a journey of roughly two hours. Diane's children—Cheryl, age eight, and Christopher, age four—sat in the back seat, weary from their trip to the big city.

The crossing of the George Washington Bridge opened a panorama of spectacular views of the Hudson River. New York City almost seemed to be too much to take in for Christopher and Cheryl, as their little town of Old Forge, near Scranton, Pennsylvania, was nothing like all the things the siblings had seen on this warm, pleasant Saturday.

The drive toward home on Route 80 West became somber as Diane's car continued through the urban morass of New Jersey. The ride home became more depressing as Route 80 sliced through the center of urban blight that was Paterson, New Jersey. Diane and Linda Jo could only look and feel pity for the residents of this blighted city they were driving through. Friends and family back in Old Forge even had an expression for people and places that seemed down on their luck and were somehow cursed to misfortune: "snakebitten."

The term *snakebitten* once again came to mind as the travelers ascended the steep grades of the Pocono Mountains into Gouldsboro, Pennsylvania. Gouldsboro, founded in the 1860s by notorious financier Jay Gould, appeared to be cursed, as the small community's weather, no matter what time of year, seemed to be symbolic of its founder's financial shenanigans—dark and cloudy. What had been a sunny day became one of clouds and mist when they reached Gouldsboro. Gouldsboro surely appeared as though it was a place "snakebitten."

The spirits of Diane, Linda Jo and the children perked up when the weather cleared dramatically as they descended Route 380 into the Lackawanna River Valley toward Scranton, Pennsylvania. Scranton was the sixth-largest city in Pennsylvania and was the Lackawanna County seat. Scrantonians, as the residents of the city proudly proclaimed themselves, called their community the "Electric City," paying homage to the fact that Scranton had electric lighting ahead of other cities in the United States.

The bright sunshine broke through the clouds and glistened on Scranton, and the optimistic nickname of the "Electric City" almost constituted a façade that belied the economic decline and rise in crime that enveloped the city. Throughout 1981, the Scranton newspapers told of crime in the city and continuously reported on the unsolved murder of Scranton School Board member Tommy Genova, shot execution-style while he was exiting his car in the parking lot of the School District's Administration Building. For many Scrantonians during 1981, the question became: was it their city or only poor Tommy Genova who was "snakebitten"?

During the 1950s, the anthracite coal industry, the economic lifeblood on which the towns of the Lackawanna County had depended for prosperity, spiraled into a long and slow period of decline. Until the 1950s, anthracite was the preferred home heating source in the United States.

The widespread use of home heating oil and natural gas began to kill the anthracite coal industry. The January 22, 1959 Knox Mine disaster in Pittston, just across the county line in Luzerne County, south of Old Forge, effectively wiped out the most viable remnants of the anthracite coal industry with the waters of the Susquehanna River flooding the interconnected mining shafts for good and drowning eighty-five coal miners in the process. Residents of Lackawanna County, speaking of the miners, whose bodies were never recovered, spoke of the lost men as "snakebitten."

The drive took its final leg toward home when Diane Ziemba got off at the Davis Street Exit from Route 81 in the Minooka section of Scranton. After passing the Sacred Heart Catholic Cemetery and the adjacent St. Joseph's Cemetery, the Ziemba car passed Colliery Avenue, a road with a notorious past. On November 1, 1973, thirteen-year-old Edmund Freach and twelve-year-old Thomas Keen were abducted and murdered within sight of their Colliery Avenue homes by William Wright, a paroled man who

Cheryl Lynn Ziemba and her brother, Christopher, July 27, 1981. *From the Scranton Times, via the Lackawanna County Historical Society.*

was an employee of a local pest control company that did work for the City of Scranton. The "Freach-Keen murders" traumatized the residents of Lackawanna County and were still an ongoing topic of conversation. Edmund Freach and Paul Keen were buried together at St. Joseph's Cemetery within a few hundred yards of their Colliery Avenue neighborhood. In years that followed the notorious murders, many residents of Old Forge would shake their heads when passing through Minooka and say, with a grim certainty, that Colliery Avenue was a place "snakebitten."

Diane Ziemba decided as an extra treat to stop off at a church picnic on this final part of the trip home. Seeing and playing with cousins Joseph Ziemba and Tracey Ziemba at a church picnic almost exceeded the fun had in New York as far as Cheryl and Christopher were concerned. Christopher, "Chrissy," as the Ziemba cousins called him, was a ball of four-year-old energy at the picnic, consuming snacks and playing with equal zeal. Despite how much Christopher was enjoying himself, Diane Ziemba soon decided that the long day should end and it was time to go home.

Diane continued to drive the car through Taylor and then into Old Forge, finally arriving home at 191 Drakes Lane in the Connell's Patch neighborhood of Old Forge. Connell's Patch had been established as a miner's village in the 1800s by the Connell Coal Company. Anthracite coal mines were known locally as "workings." Connell's Patch had been the miner's community for the Connell Coal Company's "working." The little miner's communities built in the vicinity of the "workings" were known locally as "patches."

Rough conditions in the workings, low wages and poor treatment of employees by management had led more than a few of the hardworking Irish immigrant coal miners to form secret societies against the coal companies known as the "Molly Maguires" during the 1870s. A long period of open warfare broke out in the workings and patches pitting the Molly Maguires against Pinkerton detectives hired by the coal companies as well as against local vigilantes.

Murder was a favored tactic of both the Molly Maguires and the Pinkerton detectives. Several of the more notorious members of Molly Maguires were eventually arrested, put on trial and hanged for murder. For some unfortunate members of the Molly Maguires, the formality of a trial was dispensed with, and their demise came by the rope of lynch mobs.

Stories of the feats or crimes (depending on the storytellers' sympathies) of the Molly Maguires were still being told one hundred years later in Lackawanna County. Those residents hearing the age-old tales of oppressed immigrant workers taking the law into their own hands certainly thought that the Molly Maguires who met their fate on the gallows or by the ropes of vigilantes were "snakebitten."

Much of the open ground in the Connell's Patch section of Old Forge had a darkish black color, much like the burnt cork with which the Molly Maguires darkened their faces, the result of more than one hundred years of coal mining. Piles and even large hills of a shiny, slate-like coal waste called "culm" bisected Connell's Patch. A large hill of culm waste with ghostly white birch trees growing from the jet-black earth known in the neighborhood as "Corey Slope" was a stone's throw away from the Ziembas' backyard.

During the 1920s and the 1930s, the local Scranton Mafia gangs waged war against each other much like the Molly Maguires and the Pinkerton detectives had sixty years before. All sides in these local gang wars found the old mining areas of Connell's Patch a convenient place to dump bodies. There was one particularly gruesome instance of bodies from local Mafia war victims found at the bottom of an old mine shaft that was still spoken about. In March 1934, a worker at the Pittston Company Coal Mine in Old Forge discovered three bodies at the bottom of a mine shaft entrapped in ice.

Eventually, after much effort, the bodies of Scranton hoodlums Joseph Moran, Gene Mitchell and Lester Levinson were extracted from their extrajudicial graves, still dressed in high-quality suits, with silk handkerchiefs complete with expensive pocket watches. While the bodies were recovered, no one was ever charged with the murder of the three men found in the mine shaft near Smith and Hoover Streets. Old Forge residents, when speaking of this occurrence of the old days, would shrug and say that the men were "snakebitten."

Remnants of the long-dead anthracite coal industry seemingly haunted the Connell's Patch neighborhood decades after the demise of the coal industry in Old Forge, in the form of massive abandoned wooden coal breakers and concrete coal bunkers. On January 29, 1969, the long-disused Kehoe-Berge Coal Breaker burned in a spectacular fire that in turn threatened the homes of Connell's Patch, leaving the panicked neighborhood residents to wonder whether some ghost from the area's mining past had somehow deemed them to be "snakebitten."

The foreboding history of the Connell's Patch was of no concern to Christopher Ziemba. The blond-haired little boy had loved the trip to New York, the clothes that his aunt had bought him on the trip and the church picnic. Above all other things, Christopher Ziemba loved the comic book character Superman. Christopher's aunt had bought him, in New York, Superman tights and a Superman T-shirt. There was nothing like the Superman shirt in the Gladstein's Store on Main Street in Old Forge, where Christopher's mother usually bought his clothes.

The evening was starting to set in, and Christopher and his sister, Cheryl, wanted to continue to play in the backyard. Cheryl was thrilled to be wearing a pair of new leather sandals her aunt had bought her in New York. The children were reluctant to stop their activities for the evening. Cheryl and Christopher were told that there "would always be more time to play" and that they would have a "wonderful time playing all day on Sunday."

The time for Christopher and Cheryl to play was less than anyone could have guessed. No one realized, as the fading light of the midsummer Saturday settled over Connell's Patch, was that Christopher and Cheryl were also "snakebitten."

STENCH

Fifteen-year-old Joseph Aulisio was never interested in sports. It was only by the lure of the promise of kegs of beer at a softball tournament at Old Forge's Eagle-McClure Hose Fire Company that his older brother Bobby could persuade him to attend. Sports not only did not interest Joseph Aulisio—sports bored him. In fact, Joseph Aulisio disliked sports and hated the kids who participated except for his brother.

It would be far better, from Joseph Aulisio's perspective, to spend a Sunday afternoon working on cars. After the first game of the tournament had ended, "Joey"—as friends, family and neighbors called him—convinced Bobby to drive him back home to the Villa Trailer Park.

Working on cars was, in fact, the one bright spot Joey Aulisio had in his relationship with his father. Joey could take apart just about any automobile engine and put it back together. Joey's father even bought an old 1971 Plymouth Cricket from his uncle for him. Joey was able to get the car running again and painted the car an off-white color that reminded neighbors of a refrigerator. Joey even cut a piece of white shag carpet that his dad had given him to fit to the little car's dashboard.

Carpentry was something else at which Joey Aulisio excelled. Joey built a log cabin on the property with logs he hauled with the little Cricket automobile from the Corey Slope culm bank. Joey was not old enough to drive legally, yet he drove the Cricket around the neighborhood anyway. Joey was also not supposed to tap a wire into the power line pole adjacent to his family's property, but he did so anyway. How Joey managed to tap into

Log cabin built by Joey Aulisio. *Lackawanna County District Attorney.*

the power line without electrocuting himself was itself a feat just short of a miracle. Thus, Joey's log cabin, which he called his "bunk," had both electric lights and a television. A neighbor, Doreen Propersi, during the spring gave Joey an old blue carpet, which gave his "bunk" the added luxury of wall-to-wall carpeting.

Robert "Bob" Aulisio Sr. awoke on July 26, 1981, from a Sunday afternoon's nap as Joey came into the Aulisio trailer home on Seaman Lane in the Connell's Patch neighborhood of Old Forge. Joey fetched a tool and went to the "new house" Bob had been building on the property he owned behind the trailer. Bob got up, looked out the back window of the trailer and peered through a light rain at the home he had been building for the last ten years. The truth was that the "new house" was just about the last dream Bob Aulisio had left. It was hard to fathom how just a few years before, while working on the house, Bob's friend Old Forge High School Vice Principal Walter Ermolovich called the Aulisios the "Million Dollar Family."

Walter had dropped by the Aulisio trailer to help Bob put the roof on the new house back in 1975 and admonished Bob for having young Joey up on the roof working with them. "I'm not keen on roofs myself," said Bob, but the "boy is like a shadow—he follows me everywhere." Joey was such a well-behaved child. Walter said, "Bob, if you ever wanted to give the boy up, I would adopt him in a minute."

The Aulisio family began to "unravel," according to members of the family, with the death of Bob's baby daughter Maria in 1976. The little girl was born with a heart defect and spent most of her short, tragic life at St. Christopher's Children's Hospital in Philadelphia. Bob's wife, Claire, a nurse by profession, stayed at the hospital with Maria, while he drove each day after his biology teaching duties at Lakeland High School to see his little girl. Maria's illness strained the family's finances to the point that fellow teachers at Lakeland High School collected money to cover Bob's gasoline expense for travel down to Philadelphia. Since both Bob and Claire spent each evening at Maria's bedside, the couple's boys—Bobby, Joey, Patrick, Dominick and Mike—were left to fend for themselves. It was not a good situation.

Life for the Aulisio family deteriorated further when Maria passed away. While other Old Forge families happily celebrated the bicentennial at a massive parade held on Main Street on July 4, 1976, the Aulisio family was in a state of chaos and dysfunction. Joey seemed to take Maria's death especially hard, becoming quiet, moody and aggressive. Bobby, Joey, Patrick, Dominick and Mike all served as pallbearers at Maria's funeral, an event that seemed to cast a cloud of gloom and despair over the Aulisio family—one that never left.

Maria's death left Claire an emotional wreck, unable to be a wife to Bob or a mother to the boys. To supplement the family finances, Bob took a part-time job at the Sears store in nearby Moosic. Soon, Bob began having an affair with a coworker named Phyllis. Bob spent more and more time away from home, and when he did come home, terrible fights with Claire erupted. In an ugly incident around Christmas 1978, the police were called after Bob

Aulisio house from Corey Slope. *Lackawanna County District Attorney.*

beat Claire in a flash of what one of the Aulisio boys later described as a "Jekyll and Hyde" personality. Divorce was the result of the Christmas 1978 incident, with Claire moving out of the trailer home, never to return, with the three youngest boys to live in Scranton, while Joey and Bobby remained with Bob.

It seemed, during the preceding year, that Bob Aulisio had lost touch with his boys, Joey in particular. Joey started using drugs, and at one point Bob had called him "a pot smoking cocksucker" in front of his son's friends. Joey's friends—J.R. Davis, Kenny Comcowich and Robert Colburn—in turn considered Bob Aulisio a "creep."

Early in 1981, Walter Ermolovich was back visiting the Aulisio trailer, not as a friend but rather as a vice principal concerned with the high absenteeism of Bobby and Joey. Walter was accompanied by some of the school's other teachers, who shared the concern for the boys' wellbeing. The men also expressed deep concern when Bobby and Joey did attend school, as the boys would dress in the same worn clothes and sneakers for days on end. Classmates had begun to call Joey "Stench." Less sympathetic teachers had begun to sarcastically refer to Joey as "Ace" due to his failing marks.

These revelations shocked Bob, since he had recently brought Bobby and Joey out shopping to spend a couple paychecks on brand-new shirts, pants and shoes. It all proved more than Bob could take, and he quickly lost his temper at the situation.

Bob raced around the trailer, pulling the new clothes, many still wrapped, from the boys' dressers and piling them in front of Walter and the other teachers. "These are the shirts that Bobby and Joey picked out," Bob yelled. He then picked up and threw a brand-new work boot at Bobby, which missed the boy but succeeded in shattering the trailer's sliding glass door. Bob lunged at Joey but was stopped when Walter grabbed him before he got a good hold on the teenager, thus allowing the boy to escape out the door.

Ermolovich and Bob Aulisio had previously devised a plan to keep Joey and Bobby in school by driving them directly to school each morning when Bob was on his way to his own teaching duties. What seemed to be a good plan soon proved to be unworkable, for as soon as Bob would drop the boys off at school, Bobby and Joey would run out the back door of the building and back home to do whatever they pleased.

Joey, it seemed, had also lost all fear of Bob and just about any other human being. He was becoming very aggressive toward neighbors and classmates at school. In the Connell's Patch neighborhood, Joey was reported to the police, accused of stealing bicycles.

There had been a very ugly incident at the beginning of the summer involving Joey and a Little League coach who was practicing with his team on the baseball field just across Hard Street from the new house. Joey stood at the top of Corey Slope, rolling old truck tires down the hill, along with throwing rocks and bottles down at the Little League baseball players he so hated. Several of the young ballplayers were injured by debris raining down from the Corey Slope. Before the rock throwing, Joey drove his car all over the ballfield, making deep ruts in the infield.

Little League coach Santo Tangerlia, a burly man in his fifties, had enough of this Aulisio punk. Tangerlia grabbed Joey to put a stop to his attack, ordering him to get a rake from his property and rake out the ruts he had made on the infield. Instead of bringing back a rake, Joey Aulisio came charging across Hard Street trying to hit Tangerlia with a sledgehammer. Luckily, Bob was able to run across the street and intervene before Joey got hurt or injured the coach.

Since the beginning of the summer, neighbors had been coming to Bob and blaming anything bad that happened in the neighborhood on Joey. Joey was blamed for killing cats. Joey was blamed in the trailer park for fireworks going off at all hours. Neighborhood kids claimed that Joey blew up a baby possum he had caught with an M-80 firecracker. Mr. Orlando, who lived up on Drakes Lane, kept farm animals in a small barn and claimed that Joey was coming by his property and throwing rocks at and tormenting his donkey.

The situation with his sons had gone from bad to worse for Bob Aulisio. Neighbors would whisper, in hushed tones, that the entire Aulisio family was "snakebitten."

A SUMMER SUNDAY AFTERNOON

Chester Ziemba, "Cookie" as he was known, settled down for a short nap on Sunday afternoon, July 26, 1981. Cookie would be going back to work for the night shift as a security guard, so some sleep now was necessary to get through his duties later. It already had been a long day. On his way home from the previous night's work, Cookie provided his brother-in-law some help on a plumbing job. Finally, when Cookie returned to his home on Drakes Lane in Old Forge, he found that he would have to watch Cheryl and Christopher for a while as his wife, Diane, needed to do some shopping. Soon enough, Diane came home from her shopping trip up to Kmart in Moosic, where she had gone with her sister. Belatedly, Cookie finally got the opportunity to rest.

The Ziembas lived in the upstairs apartment of a two-family stucco home at 191 Drakes Lane in the Connell's Patch neighborhood. Cookie and Diane moved into their apartment the previous winter, renting from their downstairs neighbor, Doreen Propersi. Cookie and Diane Ziemba found their new home a suitable arrangement, since it provided the privacy the couple lacked when they resided with Cookie's parents. Doreen, the Ziembas' landlord and neighbor, and her boyfriend, Lenny Brown, had become good friends with Diane and Cookie.

Diane and Cookie Ziemba were Old Forge natives, surrounded by extended family settled in the various neighborhoods of the borough. The Ziembas loved their small-town life. In the summers, watermelons were sold out of the back of a truck from street to street by one enterprising man.

The Aulisio "new house" as it appears today. *Brian Kincaid.*

One of the high school teachers sold bleach out of his car. Diane bought children's books for Cheryl at Cherri's bookstore on Main Street, and Cookie would buy Superman comic books for Christopher at Sambo's variety store. Sambo's was so crowded with wall-to-wall merchandise that it would bring a smile to Cookie's face when the owner of the store would comment to him on the volume of goods for sale and would say, "I don't sell space."

Doreen Propersi always went out of her way to help neighbors and took it upon herself to feed the Aulisio boys dinner on most evenings. Doreen's kitchen was the scene of endless card games between Cookie, Lenny and Bobby Aulisio. Joey Aulisio, quieter than his brother Bobby, did not partake in the card games but was content to just sit and watch the goings-on in Doreen's kitchen.

Directly behind 191 Drakes Lane sprawled the Villa Trailer Park, with its intersecting streets of Seaman Lane and Hard Street. Corey Slope stood at the end of Hard Street. Corey Slope rose in a somber manner above the surrounding neighborhood and acted as a border between the neighborhood and the vast wilderness of heavily wooded mountains, and abandoned anthracite mines, to the southwest.

Cheryl and Christopher quickly found friends among the many children of the nearby trailer park, and they were particularly fond of Joe and Linda

Lilli's little girl, Jessica. The Aulisio boys were looked up to as friends by the Ziemba children.

Cookie and Lenny found that Joey Aulisio was a handy kid to have around since he could fix just about any problem either they or the men had with their pickup trucks. Joey also cut Doreen's lawn for her and helped with carpentry projects around her home.

The rain seemed to have subsided, and the kids asked Cookie if they could go outside and play. "If it's alright with your mother," Cookie replied to his children, who then turned to Diane for permission. Diane scanned the apartment, noting that the kids had cleaned their room, and then checked the children's attire. Cheryl wore a red tank top along with red shorts and sandals that had been purchased on Saturday's trip to New York City. Chris was wearing his prized Superman T-shirt with blue stretch pants from the trip along with rubber flip-flops. Noting that it was already a quarter to four, Diane said to Cheryl, "Make sure you and your brother be back by five o'clock for dinner." The two children scrambled down the stairs and jumped onto their bikes. Within a minute, Cheryl and Chris were knocking on the door of Joe Lilli's trailer on Seaman Lane, only to be told by Mr. Lilli that his daughter, Jessica, was out with her mother.

Joe Lilli stammered as he spoke to the Ziemba children. Cheryl did not know that the reason for Mr. Lilli's funny way of talking was due to the stroke he had suffered. Joe Lilli decided to get himself an early dinner at Snack and Putt, a combination miniature golf course and hot dog stand near where Main Street crossed over the Pennsylvania Turnpike. Cheryl and Christopher moved on from the Lilli trailer, looking for other kids to play with.

Sandra Davis wanted a little time for herself and delayed going food shopping until the Sunday afternoon movie on television was over. Even though the stores would close at five o'clock, Sandra waited until her movie ended at 3:30 p.m. to get ready to go out. On her way out of her trailer home, Sandra looked up at the clock and noticed that it was 3:45 p.m. Walking to her car, Sandra noticed the Ziemba children riding bikes past her trailer.

Even if Jessica Lilli was not home, there were more possibilities of playmates in the trailer park for Cheryl and Christopher. The siblings rode their bikes down to the Aulisio property, where Patrick Aulisio, who was visiting with his father for the weekend, was sitting in his father's old green jeep with J.R. Davis. Would the boys let Cheryl and Christopher play with them in the jeep? The answer from Patrick Aulisio was "No." Christopher was upset that the bigger boys would not let him play in the jeep. Cheryl took her brother and looked for other possibilities to play.

The jeep on the Aulisio property. *Lackawanna County District Attorney.*

Sandra Davis pulled her car up to the jeep. Mrs. Davis was not about to have J.R. wandering around the neighborhood while she was out. Lately, J.R.'s friend Joey Aulisio had been accused of stealing bikes around the neighborhood. In fact, Joey was being blamed for just about anything that went wrong in Connell's Patch. Simply no good would come of J.R. running around with Joey while Sandra was not home.

No, it would be far better for J.R. to be inside the trailer while Mrs. Davis was gone. Sandra instructed her son to go into the trailer and watch TV while she was gone, telling J.R. that he could bring Patrick in the trailer with him. J.R. Davis settled down in his family's trailer to watch a western. At least Patrick Aulisio was with him to help pass the time.

How about a game of cops and robbers in the new house Mr. Aulisio was building? The cops and robbers game sure sounded like fun to Cheryl and Christopher. Oh, how the inside of the new house echoed when Cheryl and Christopher yelled and screamed during the game. There was even an old wooden baby's highchair to play in. What fun it was as Cheryl and Christopher jumped up and down, running around yelling in the new house.

"Hands up!" was yelled from across the room. Suddenly there was the flash of blue light. There was smoke. The loud explosion from the shotgun echoed throughout the new house.

Survival instincts kicked in for Cheryl Ziemba. Was it real what she just saw? There was no escape out the back of the new house. The front door was boarded over, and the garage door was closed. Somebody must have heard it. Someone must be coming over to the new house to help. The only thing to do was to run and hide. A primal fear came over the little girl. Running up the stairs of the new house, Cheryl hid in the back bedroom closet. Up the stairs came the echoes of footsteps. The footsteps went from room to room. The folding doors of the closet opened. Cheryl was crouching with her head in the corner of the closet. Another flash of blue light lit up the closet interior, and a second blast from a shotgun reverberated throughout the rear bedroom.

On the porch of his trailer at the corner of Olivia Street and Hard Street, Billy McHugh heard the first blast. Firecrackers again? McHugh had just about had it with his neighbor's kid, Joey Aulisio, who had been setting off firecrackers all summer. A second blast drew Billy McHugh's attention toward the new house that Bob Aulisio was building next door. Billy McHugh then turned toward his wife and said, "There he goes again."

What had just happened? How could this have happened? Panic set in. This could not have happened. This did not happen. He did not do this. Blood, hair and pieces of brain were everywhere. This was trouble. This was more trouble than he ever knew. It seemed to him, as he would later say, "fucking disgusting." He was, as he would later say, "in denial." There was only one thing to do: clean it up before he got into trouble.

THE MOUNTAIN

Alan Hoover and Tom Scoda checked out of work at Fitchburg Coated Products at 3:00 p.m. on July 26, 1981. The Sunday shift was always extra money, so working on a weekend was not so tragic.

What was nearly tragic was the accident Tom's brother had the night before, which banged him up enough to put him in the hospital. So, the first order of business was to stop at the garage and pick up the cassette tapes from his brother's car before they were stolen.

Then it was off to the main chore of the day: Tom and Alan had to pick up the brush from Alan's yard in Duryea, just south of Old Forge, and dump it up on the mountain near Connell's Patch. Tom drove up the back way on the dirt road that led up the mountain as a light drizzle fell. The mountain consisted of thick green woodlands, long-abandoned strip mining pits and, above all else, pile upon pile of culm from which stark birch trees grew.

Finally, they reached their destination, the abandoned stripping pit where the dirt road divided, with one section heading in a southerly direction to Connell Street in Old Forge and the other heading farther up the mountain. Tom backed the truck to the edge of the pit to dump the brush out of the pickup truck's rear. Tom checked his watch, and it was nearly 4:50 p.m.

Alan Hoover was a man who liked to pay attention to detail. Current events and the news were his passion. Alan Hoover spent hours clipping newspaper articles of what he deemed newsworthy or important. When singer John Lennon was assassinated the previous winter, Alan made sure to save the newspaper articles. Hoover's brother was a sailor on the aircraft

carrier USS *Nimitz*, and he always made sure to save articles pertaining to the ship and its voyages.

Hoover looked down the dirt mountain road in the direction of Old Forge in the valley below. Even as a child, Alan paid attention to current events and remembered how, in 1969, Old Forge held a parade for Glynn Lunney, an Old Forge native who served as the flight director at Mission Control for the moon landing.

Opposite: Rough terrain up the mountain road, July 28, 1981. *Lackawanna County District Attorney.*

Above: The 1971 Plymouth Cricket used to dump the bodies. *Lackawanna County District Attorney.*

Tom Scoda's interest was all things automotive. Scoda could tell by the look of any vehicle the manufacturer, the year and model. Accordingly, as the men dumped the brush from Scoda's pickup truck into the pit, the conversation alternated from current events to cars.

Suddenly, there was the sound of a car's engine struggling to climb up the mountain road from Old Forge. A small white car crested the hill, driven by what seemed to be a kid wearing thick glasses. The men were shocked that such a small car could climb the road. The kid seemed startled to see them. The kid in the car passed by with both men staring at the odd-looking vehicle.

After unloading the brush, the pair decided to drive up the mountain, as Alan Hoover was curious to see how bad the gypsy moth infestation had been that summer. Tom Scoda began to pull his pickup truck away from the pit when he again had to pull over to the side of the road to let the little white car pass by; it was now traveling down the mountain. Tom looked intently at the little vehicle's front grill since he had never seen a car of this type before. Alan Hoover watched the white car as it drove at a high rate of speed down the narrow dirt road with what appeared to be some sort of cloth hanging out of the trunk. "I would rip out the bottom of the car

31

if I drove like that," Hoover said. "That was weird to see a car like that up here," Tom Scoda commented.

Sandra Davis noticed that it was 5:30 p.m. when she got back home from shopping. Davis was more than a little proud of herself that she managed to watch her movie and get the shopping done. She now made J.R. a fast, "real slick" dinner. She noticed the clock again as her son finished his meal and bounded out the trailer door around 5:45 p.m.; she watched him run over to the Aulisio property to ride a minibike with the Aulisio boys.

"LINDA JO, DID I leave my wallet in your car?" Diane Ziemba asked her sister over the phone, hoping that she would say Cheryl and Christopher were there with her. Linda Jo quickly checked her car and called back on the phone, "It's not there, Diane."

Diane hung up the phone and immediately called her sister back, telling Linda Jo that Cheryl and Christopher were missing and that she had hoped they may have wandered down to her house. Diane told her sister that she had just gone door to door in the trailer park to locate the children without success.

Diane had hoped when Cheryl and Christopher had not come home for dinner that the kids had just lost track of time. Diane now found herself in a panic, as it was quite unlike her children to just wander off like this. Cookie was walking around the neighborhood searching for the children. Having sensed the panic in her sister's voice, Linda Jo immediately headed down to Diane's with her husband to help search for Chris and Cheryl.

Cookie had gone from house to house on Drakes Lane and trailer to trailer in the trailer park. At each door, Cookie was told that no one had seen the children. Cookie kept yelling out Cheryl's and Christopher's names, but no voices answered his calls. This was so unlike either child. Cookie knew that wherever they were, the kids had to be together, as Cheryl would never leave her brother to wander on his own.

After an hour of looking around the neighborhood, Cookie turned up not a sign of either Cheryl or Christopher. It was almost six o'clock. Surely the children must be hungry. Clearly, Cookie needed help in finding the children. Luckily, Bobby Aulisio had just come home from his softball game and could help him search. Bobby Aulisio and his brother Joey knew their way around the neighborhood better than anyone, Cookie thought. If there was some place the children could have run off to, surely either Bobby or Joey would know of it. Cookie walked up to the Aulisio trailer and yelled, "Hey Bobby, I need your help."

"Where's your brother?" Bob Aulisio said to Joey, scowling. "He's not back from the ballgame yet," Joey said. It was now 5:45 p.m., and Bob was livid, as he had specifically told Bobby to be back home at 5:30 p.m. "I'm going over to get him—give me the keys to the Cricket," Bob Aulisio snapped back. "You can't take the Cricket, Dad; the oil pan is busted," Joey said.

Bob's anger overcame the fact that the car was damaged, and he blurted, "I don't care I'm taking it anyway." Then he drove the little automobile over to the ballfield. Bob was stewing over why the Cricket's oil pan was busted, as he had just driven the car the night before and it seemed fine. The Cricket seemed to Bob to be in the same place he had parked when he got home the night before, so how could the oil pan now be broken? Bobby was already driving out of the parking lot at the ballfield when his father caught up with him. Pulling alongside his son's car, Bob yelled over, "Get your ass home!"

Kenny Comcowich had been working all afternoon attempting to get his car in running order. Kenny's car was a work in progress, and it looked as though he would finally be able to finish the getting the vehicle running.

When Kenny's mother came home from the afternoon shift at the nursing home, at 5:30 p.m., he had her drive him down to Capp's filling station to buy a few jugs of gasoline. Kenny lacked a funnel to put the gas in his car. Luckily, the answer to Kenny's dilemma was close at hand since his good friend Joey Aulisio lived only a short distance away. Joey always had a good supply of tools and auto parts on hand. Kenny guessed that Joey's house would be the best place he could get his hands on a gas funnel.

Kenny's mother dropped him off in front of the house that Mr. Aulisio was building. This was where Joey usually could be found. Kenny walked up to the garage door and looked through the window. Joey, shirtless and his chest coated with sweat, came walking into the garage from the upstairs of the house. "Hey Joey, do you have a gas funnel that I can borrow?" Ken yelled into the garage. Joey seemed startled by Kenny's presence and for a moment just stared through his thick glasses at his friend.

J.R. Davis came walking up to the door with Joey's brother Patrick. Davis glanced into the garage and yelled, "Hey Joey, are you working in there?" "Yes, J.R. I'm working," Joey replied, looking upset. Joey then turned toward the garage door window, looking at Kenny, and said, "There's a funnel around here somewhere." It was at this point that Kenny Comcowich noticed the pool of blood on the concrete pad in front of the garage sticking out from under the hood from a Ford Pinto. J.R. Davis noticed the blood as well. Joey's brother Patrick came around from the side

The garage at the Aulisio "new house," July 27, 1981. *Lackawanna County District Attorney.*

of the house with the funnel Kenny wanted. Pointing down to the pool of blood, J.R. yelled into the garage, "Hey Joey, who got cut?" "I did," Joey responded.

VOLUNTEER FIRE DEPARTMENTS WERE a major part of the fabric of social life in the Lackawanna Valley in 1981. Aside from the actual fighting of fires, there were many picnics, parades, competitions and carnivals held by each volunteer "hose" every year, filling up the social calendars of the membership.

In 1981, the popularity of the "hoses" often resulted in many of Lackawanna County's towns and boroughs being served by more than one volunteer fire company. Old Forge was served by three volunteer "hoses": "Old Forge," "White-Eagle-McClure" and "Lawrenceville."

Old Forge is situated on the banks of the Lackawanna River just south of Scranton. Many of Old Forge's neighborhoods date back to the borough's coal mining past with names like Snyder's Patch, Bush Patch and Connell's Patch, named for the coal companies that once worked the land. Other neighborhoods of the borough had almost whimsical names such as Goose Alley, Babylon and Barbertown.

During the summer of 1981, troubles plagued the community of 9,230 inhabitants. There had been an alarming number of gang fights between the teenagers of Old Forge. It seemed each street in the borough had its own gang. The gangs did not fight over drug money or other illicit activities but rather for "turf" and over girls. The "George Street Gang" was reported to be the toughest of the gangs. One such gang fight resulted in the death of fifty-nine-year-old Joseph Whah, who had fallen, hitting his head on a sidewalk, after being punched in the face by a teenager while trying to break up the fight.

More bad news was yet to come when, in early 1981, polychlorinated biphenyls, commonly referred to as "PCBs," were discovered on the property of the Lehigh Electric and Engineering Company in town. Residents of Old Forge were clearly worried in the summer of 1981 that their drinking water was being contaminated from the toxic site, which sat atop the mountain to the west of the borough.

Given the gang fights of the past year and the discovery of a toxic waste site on the mountain, it would not have been difficult in the summer of 1981 to find members of the Old Forge Hose volunteer firehouse on Main Avenue who would agree that their community was "snakebitten." However, the firefighters present on this Sunday evening, July 26, 1981, would have no such negative talk, as the day, though cloudy with light rain at times, had been a good one. It was just about time to call it a night after the three games of softball, which the Old Forge Hose's team had won at the White-Eagle firehouse in the Bush Patch neighborhood.

Stanley "Stosh" Zoltewicz, Mike Nalevanko, Ed Orzalek and seventeen-year-old junior firefighter Frank Genell came back to the firehouse to put some time in on their pet project. The four men had been engaged for the past year in building a four-wheel-drive mini-pumper fire engine nearly from scratch, building on a Ford heavy-duty pickup truck chassis, while their wives and girlfriends attended the Sunday night ladies' auxiliary meeting. The group hoped that the mini-pumper, painted in an eye-catching black lacquer, rather than the traditional fire service red, would be a prize winner at the many parades held each summer.

The fire station of the Old Forge Hose shared its quarters with the Old Forge Borough Hall and police department downtown along Main Street. A large 155mm howitzer, a relic salvaged from World War II, greeted visitors at the municipal complex. On Friday nights, for some unexplained reason, the teenagers of Old Forge hung out around the Borough Hall in great numbers. Although many of the firefighters of the Old Forge Hose considered all the kids to be pests, the police actually welcomed the occurrence if for no other reason than it made it much easier to keep an eye on the teenagers of Old Forge for at least one night of each weekend.

Throughout the borough, large banks of the coal mining waste product culm abounded, intersecting neighborhoods, a reminder of Old Forge's coal mining past. The culm banks, however, belied the early history of Old Forge, as much of the borough's early development was tied to iron rather than anthracite coal.

A bronze plaque in the Borough Hall told of this early iron industry history of Old Forge. In 1789, Dr. William Hooker Smith and James Sutton built the first iron forge within the present limits of Old Forge. For many years, the iron forge of Smith and Sutton prospered along the banks of the Lackawanna River. The forge was a considerable industrial operation for its time and produced pig iron.

About a decade later, the Slocum family built a forge at Slocum's Hollow, and when it went into production, the residents began to refer to Hooker and Smith's operation as "the old forge," thus giving a name to the town that grew around this early industrial enterprise.

The borough's first anthracite coal operation was the Chittenden Breaker. Soon Coal, Breakers, Workings and Miner's Patches grew throughout what became, in 1889, Old Forge Borough.

As coal mining declined, other industries arrived. Silk mills, such as Butler Silk, employed the wives of coal miners and eventually former miners. By the beginning of World War II, Maxson Electric Corporation had opened its doors in Old Forge, manufacturing electronic equipment. In what seemed to be a continued cycle of industrial boom and bust in Old Forge, both Maxson and Butler Silk both closed in the 1970s.

The many restaurants on Main Street, within walking distance of the Old Forge Hose fire station, reflected Old Forge's coal mining past, serving a menu of what became known and sought after throughout Pennsylvania as "Old Forge pizza." The pizza was cut not into pie slices but rather in rectangular pieces, with a balanced tomato sauce with a blend of cheeses, typically white American and mozzarella. The pizza type's origins dated back decades, when the Ghigiarelli family served the fare to hungry coal miners. Starting in the 1960s, restaurants specializing in Old Forge pizza such as Revello's, Arcaro & Genell, Augustine's and Ghigiarelli's established themselves on Main Street. Rarely was there parking available on Saturday nights on Main Street, such was the demand for the style.

Work on the mini-pumper was just about finished for the evening as Stosh's wife, Anna Marie, signaled to him that the ladies' auxiliary meeting was over. Just as Stosh prepared to leave, the desk duty police officer entered the fire station bays with Cookie Ziemba and Bobby Aulisio, who had been at the softball game up at the White-Eagle Hose ballfield.

The officer requested assistance of the Old Forge Hose's firefighters in finding two children who had disappeared from their home on Drakes Lane. The borough's fire siren wailed into the humid night air, and fire pagers blared out a missing person alert. Stosh, Ed, Mike and Frank mounted up in the mini-pumper and headed for Drakes Lane. Drakes Lane, named for one of Old Forge's founders, Charles Drake, ran from Main Street deep into the Connell's Patch section of Old Forge. The debate regarding whether Old Forge was indeed "snakebitten" had just been decided.

FRANTIC

 ookie Ziemba was now frantic, as the children were missing without the slightest indication of their whereabouts. Cookie was able to, with Bobby Aulisio's help, muster a search party consisting of himself, Bobby and Joey. The group first searched the top of Corey Slope and then covered the backyards of the trailer park, finding no sign of the children. Relatives began arriving to help look for the kids. Cookie's brothers formed up another search party, checking backyards of the homes along Drakes Lane. Cookie along with Joey and Bobby Aulisio checked an abandoned old concrete structure left over from the days of mining and known to local kids as "the altar" in the woods off Connell Street. There was no sign of Cheryl or Christopher at either the altar or along Drakes Lane.

With darkness setting in, Cookie and Bobby Aulisio decided that it would be best to walk down to Old Forge Borough Hall and to get help from the police. The reaction was immediate, as the borough's fire sirens began to issue a mournful wail, beckoning Old Forge's volunteer firefighters out to duty.

Sergeant Frank Biaranccardi of the Old Forge police had been in Burger King's parking lot on Main Avenue when the call came in to report to Borough Hall. Biaranccardi went first to Borough Hall, speaking with the duty officer, and then to Cookie Ziemba, who was with a large teenager he recognized as Bobby Aulisio. After conferring with Cookie and Bobby, Biaranccardi decided that it would be best for him to first go to the trailer park and get a firm grasp of the situation.

Arriving at the trailer park, Biaranccardi found a large group of teenagers gathering under the streetlight on the corner of Seaman Lane and Hard Street directly behind the Ziemba home. Biaranccardi asked the teens if anyone had seen the Ziemba children. Biaranccardi knew Joey Aulisio by sight, as he had previously investigated allegations by neighbors that Joey had been stealing bicycles and an incident of an altercation with a Little League coach.

All of the kids, except for Joey, indicated that they had last seen the children playing on an empty concrete trailer pad between the Davis and Lilli trailers. Joey Aulisio told Biaranccardi that he last seen the children at around four o'clock near the base of Corey Slope at the corner of Hard and Olivia Street. Since Joey's sighting seemed to be most recent, Biaranccardi decided that it would be best to start the search at Corey Slope.

Mike Nalevanko parked the mini-pumper in front of the Ziemba home, while Old Forge Hose's pumper crew stationed their fire engine near the base of Corey Slope. An engine from White-Eagle Hose arrived, and its crew immediately set up floodlights pointed toward the crest of Corey Slope. Mike ran up to the front porch of the Ziemba home to get descriptions of the children from their parents. Nalevanko found Diane Ziemba sitting on the porch crying and asked what the children looked like. Cheryl was described as eight years old, having shoulder-length auburn hair and wearing a red tank top, red shorts and leather sandals. Christopher was reported by Diane to have sandy blond hair, wearing a Superman T-shirt, blue stretch pants and rubber flip-flops. Christopher loved the theme from the *Superman* show on TV, so Diane gave the police a tape of the song for the police to play on their loudspeakers in the hopes that it would lure him out of the woods. Diane warned Mike that the little boy was afraid of the engine noise the fire truck made, so it would be better if the engine could be shut off.

Old Forge Police Chief Stanley Lisowski arrived to take command of the search efforts and immediately conferred with the fire chiefs of all three of Old Forge's fire companies. The fire chiefs agreed with Chief Lisowski that given the size of the area to be searched, outside help needed to be called in. Lisowski radioed out a mutual aid request to the Pennsylvania State Police and to the towns of Taylor, Moosic, Jenkins, Duryea, Ransom, Pittston and Wilkes-Barre, along with the city of Scranton.

Lawrenceville Hose Chief Hughes started his fire company's search efforts at the foot of Corey Slope. After driving up a narrow dirt path that ran from Hard Street up to the top of Corey Slope to conduct a reconnaissance, Hughes organized a search of the surrounding woods, with each searcher standing about at arm's length apart to ensure that all ground was covered in the failing light of the day.

Part-time police officer Mark Stillwagon heard commotion from his home on George Street coming from the direction of the trailer park. Walking down Drakes Lane, Stillwagon found a search effort underway at Corey Slope for two lost children. Looking at the rain-filled sky, Stillwagon knew, even though it was summer, that the skin-drenching mist would be dangerous to any children exposed to the cool night air and immediately joined the search, adding his expertise in organizing the search parties.

Incoming volunteers were instructed to report to White-Eagle Hose, which would serve as the command post. News bulletins on television had the effect of bringing out droves of searchers from all over the Lackawanna Valley to Old Forge. Nearly five hundred volunteer searchers had arrived on the scene by midnight.

SEARCHERS

Sergeant Biaranccardi selected a team of local teenagers to help search the trailer park and the surrounding woods. The sergeant picked the Aulisio boys, Bobby and Joey, to join him since they seemed to know the neighborhood better than anyone else. Although Biaranccardi was told that the altar had been checked earlier by Cookie Ziemba and the Aulisio brothers, he decided that another search of it would be wise in case the children were currently wandering in that vicinity. Next, the group checked the abandoned house on Milwaukee Avenue. Bobby Aulisio searched the top floor, while Joey yelled up the stairs for Bobby to beware of the weak floorboards. Biaranccardi was very impressed with the breadth of knowledge Joey Aulisio had for his neighborhood, as it seemed the boy knew the area to the square inch.

Doreen Propersi arrived home from a daylong clambake to find the streets surrounding her home filled with fire engines, police cars and volunteers searching for the Ziemba children. Doreen first attempted to calm Diane, who was sitting on the front porch crying softly as she stared into the rain-swept streets, as if she expected to see her children appear from the mist. Although Christopher and Cheryl were very active children, it seemed illogical to Doreen that they could wander a great distance so she suggested she would look to see if the children were somehow hiding in the house. After searching the entire house with no results, Doreen returned to the front porch to comfort Diane.

Doreen's boyfriend, Lenny Brown, began a search for the children by enlisting the help of the local CB radio club to which he belonged. Lenny reasoned that the more eyes out looking for Cheryl and Christopher, the more ground that a search could cover.

While Lenny was making calls to organize the CB search, Doreen decided it may have been possible that the kids had wandered up to the abandoned strip mining pits above Connell's Patch and got lost in its maze of trails and back roads. Doreen told Lenny to drive up to the pits in his pickup truck and take along the Aulisio boys since they knew their way on the mountain. Joey Aulisio seemed to be the real expert when it came to directions on the back roads of Connell's Patch since the boy had been hunting and fishing on the mountain since he was about ten years old.

Joey Aulisio not only excelled at local geography, but he also was an expert mechanic and carpenter. During the late spring, Doreen and Lenny cleaned the basement of the Drakes Lane house, removing several old blue carpets that had been in storage for many years. Joey, seeing the activity in Doreen's yard, came over and asked if he could have the carpets for the "bunk," a hut he had built. Joey gave Doreen a tour of his "bunk." The "bunk" turned out to be a log cabin built along the back of the Aulisio property, complete with electricity.

Doreen asked Joey where he obtained the logs for his cabin, and the teenager pointed up the mountain top, stating that he dragged the logs from the woods with his car. Doreen thought it was "neat" that a teenager could build a log cabin as Joey Aulisio did.

It was clear to Doreen that car repair was a passion of Joey's. Bob Aulisio had often bragged to Doreen that Joey had been working with automobile engines since he was a little boy. By the age of fifteen, Joey had his own car, a 1971 Plymouth Cricket, which he had rebuilt and painted. The boy would drive the auto around the trailer park and up on the mountain past the strip mining pits on fishing and hunting trips. Joey Aulisio was proud of the job he had done rebuilding and repainting his little white Plymouth Cricket. He had recently even showed off to Doreen the white shag carpet added to the Cricket's dashboard.

Joey was sitting with Diane Ziemba and his friend J.R. Davis on the front porch of Doreen's house. Diane was in hysterics at this point, so Doreen thought it best to get the boys off the porch and out to help Lenny with the search. Lenny's truck would not start, so Joey drove Bob Aulisio's jeep over to Drakes Lane to jump-start the pickup. Watching the efforts to start Lenny's pickup truck, Doreen wondered why Joey was using his father's jeep rather than his own car to power the jump-start.

With his truck now started, Lenny along with Bobby, J.R. and Joey took the pickup truck to begin the search on the mountains above Connell's Patch. A dirt road known locally as Deater's Lane ran from the end of Connell Street, past the old Connell Coal Company operation, to a point where a road that ascends the ridge to the abandoned strip mining pits begins. Lenny turned his pickup truck up the mountain lane in search of the children. About halfway up the road, a group of teenagers was found sitting on cars and drinking beer. The teens said that earlier in the day they had seen a little boy and girl pushing bikes up the road toward the stripping pits.

Having been given the sighting by the teenagers of children on the mountain road, Lenny decided to head back and pick up Cookie Ziemba to accompany the group for another search of the dirt road leading to the strip mines. Bobby Aulisio and the men sat in the front seat of the pickup, while Joey and J.R. stayed in the back of the truck. Since Joey knew the roads of the mountain better than anyone else, he shouted directions to Lenny. The mountain roads above Connell's Patch were narrow and dangerous, and one wrong turn could lead to the truck falling several hundred feet into one of the stripping pits. More than once, during the ride, Joey yelled to Lenny, "Wrong way asshole—do you want to get us all killed!?"

Periodically, Brown would stop the truck and the group would call out the children's names into the night air in hope of a response. Lenny could hear everyone in the pickup truck yelling the names of Cheryl and Christopher except for Joey, who sat silently in the pickup truck's cargo bed.

STATE TROOPERS

Children do not just wander away on their own, MaryAnne," Lieutenant Mike Jordan of the Pennsylvania State Police said to his wife as the television broadcast a news report live from Old Forge. Mike Jordan headed the Criminal Investigation Unit of Troop R at the Dunmore State Police Barracks, and he knew all too well that young children could not wander very far by themselves.

The instincts of the seasoned State Police veteran had already concluded that the Ziemba children had been abducted. Mike Jordan darkly suspected that his unit would be called to the scene before long.

"Stosh" Zoltewicz watched as searchers continued to stream into the Connell's Patch neighborhood even though it was well after midnight. The Scranton police were now on the scene with search dogs. The dogs were able to follow the children's scent from the Ziemba home to the concrete trailer pad next to the Davis family trailer. The rain eliminated the scent of the children from beyond the trailer pad.

Since it was possible that the Ziemba children could be anywhere in Old Forge, it was decided to search the entire town rather than just concentrating on Connell's Patch. Stosh with Mike, Ed and Frank brought the mini-pumper over to the Gilcrest Trucking Company to check trailers on the property, which encompassed nineteen acres on Moosic Road. It proved to be a long and physically taxing job to search the tract.

After a search of the undersides, interiors and roofs of each trailer, Mike decided that the men may have better luck elsewhere. Although it seemed a remote possibility that young children could travel so far on foot, the group decided to check the old mining roads above Connell's Patch.

Since the mini-pumper had four-wheel-drive, it was the ideal vehicle to traverse the rocky roads of the mountain. The one drawback to the mini-pumper was that it lacked the floodlights necessary to illuminate a large area. Stosh had to improvise using a handheld light. The light's beam only reached out about twenty feet. Stosh stopped the truck at each pit on the way up the mountain to have the group check these black canyons the best they could. The firefighters stopped at the pit that was second from the top of the mountain and dismounted to behold an eerie scene. Down in the valley below, they could see beams of flashlights breaking, appearing almost to be the lights of fireflies, through the night's mist marking the paths of hundreds of volunteer searchers. Voices pierced the damp air, echoing up the mountain.

Frantic shouts calling out for the missing children—"Chris, Cheryl, if you can hear us come out"—could be heard from the valley. Loudspeakers blared the *Superman* theme song that Diane Ziemba had provided to the police. The song's lyrics echoed up the mountain. Convinced that further search of the mountain would be useless while it was still dark, Stosh suggested that the group head on back to Old Forge and continue the search in town.

Once they were down the mountain, Mike drove the mini-pumper over to the White-Eagle Hose for further instructions. Their group was now assigned to begin searching the woods behind Stosh's in-laws' house, located on Milwaukee Avenue. The search of the woods continued back behind the Corey Slope to a point behind Old Forge's senior citizens housing. The searchers then penetrated the woods all the way to the wooded area behind Stosh's house on Apache Drive and the grounds of Old Forge High School.

Police Chief Lisowski, Trooper Kaczorowski and volunteer searcher Marie Skutack made a search of the Old Forge Cemetery and checked the wooded area on Butler Street near the Slavic Cemetery. A report had come in after midnight that Mrs. Febbo of Brook Street had heard a child calling for her grandmother in an alley between Humphrey and Brook Streets. Since the location of this report was close to the Ziemba home, it led to another search of the entire Connell's Patch section of Old Forge.

Back at the White-Eagle Hose, Jack Schuback was coordinating all the volunteer search groups. Another report had come in from Tom Yescavage of Monroe Street, near the Old Forge Cemetery, that he heard somebody in his backyard and turned on this spotlight. He spotted one person who yelled to another, "They are looking for us. We better run!" From this information, a search was made of the entire Moosic Road area that lasted until daybreak.

Prior to dawn, Marie Skutack and Helen Tansley searched the Popple Brothers industrial area and the banks of the Lackawanna River. Police Chief Lisowski, with Councilman Joe Lacomy, then searched Deater's Lane and traveled to the opposite end of town to check the area around the Topps Baseball Card factory. Chief Lisowski then had Diane Ziemba, who had been sitting crying on her front porch, brought down to the White-Eagle Hose command post so that she could be interviewed again for any new information that had been obtained by her in the past hours.

Stosh, Mike, Ed and Frank had been searching for the woods behind Apache Drive when, at 4:30 a.m., the word came over the radio for all searchers to report back to the command post. Since the search had been in full swing for seven hours and all the volunteers were exhausted, it was decided to conclude the search for the evening and begin again at 6:30 a.m.

THIS THING WITH THE Ziemba kids frightened Bob Aulisio. Both Bobby and Joey had been out searching in the neighborhood, and now it was beginning to get dark. Bob ordered his other sons—Patrick, Dominick and Mike—to stay on the property.

Paul Kuzara, who lived across the street from Bob Aulisio, came over to the Aulisio trailer when he saw the fire trucks arriving on Seaman Lane. Paul asked Bob what was going on and was surprised to learn that Cookie Ziemba's children were missing. Paul Kuzara inquired, "Did anyone check in the new house, Bob?" "I don't know so let's go over," Bob Aulisio replied. The pair entered the new house from the unlocked back door and yelled out for Cheryl and Christopher. There was no answer or any sign of the Ziemba children. Kuzara noticed a heavy smell of gasoline throughout the new house, which he assumed was from Joey working on cars in the garage.

Patrolman Henry Wylam, a former football star for the Old Forge High School Blue Devils, had been one of the first members of the police department to respond to the missing children alert. High school football had a long legacy in Old Forge, and as a former star player, Wylam was well known throughout the community. Old Forge's downtown was crowded on Friday nights in the fall for the high school football games, played under lights at the stadium just east of Main Street.

After a few hours of searching and taking statements from people in the neighborhood, Wylam organized a search of the new house Bob Aulisio was building. The search party consisting of Wylam along with Cookie Ziemba's brothers, Leonard and Robert, entered the two-floor structure through the unlocked garage door at about 12:45 a.m. Since there was no electric power in the new house, the group had to rely on two handheld flashlights. Wylam along with Cookie's brothers went through the garage and to the upstairs as far as the hallway. There was a strong smell of gasoline throughout the house. Leonard Ziemba shined his flashlight at the kitchen, admiring the workmanship of the construction and stating, "Bob really did a nice job on this house."

Although the search for the children had been called off for the night and was not to resume until 6:30 a.m., firefighter Louis Materazzi of the Old Forge Hose could not sleep and arrived back at the trailer park at around 5:30 a.m. Monday morning, July 27, 1981. Walking up toward Corey Slope, Materazzi noticed two teenagers sitting in a green jeep that was parked on the Aulisio property. Joey Aulisio was lying in the back of the jeep, while the other kid was now standing alongside of it. It did not seem right for two young kids to be out at this late hour. "Joey, what are you doing outside at this hour?" Materazzi asked. Joey replied, "Helping with the search." "Well, it's a little late, shouldn't you be in the house? You should be at home sleeping," Materazzi replied.

Joey answered, "If I go in the trailer my father will kill me for going in so late." Materazzi continued his search. Materazzi checked the new house Bob Aulisio was building. The back door itself was unlocked. Afraid to enter the building and trespass, Materazzi stuck his head in the back door and yelled the names of the Ziemba children. As a firefighter, Materazzi took note of the strong smell of gasoline coming from the house.

Frank and Diane LaSota had been searching all night when they decided to take a break and head home at 4:00 a.m. Rather than trying to sleep, the LaSotas decided to have coffee before heading back to the trailer park to continue searching. They arrived back on Hard Street at 6:00 a.m. to find that the search parties had not yet begun the morning search. The LaSotas decided to begin the search on their own, following the dirt road up Corey Slope.

After walking up the dirt road two hundred feet, Frank LaSota noticed a blue piece of carpet. Since it had been raining for most of the night, it seemed conceivable that the children could have hidden under the carpet as shelter from the storm. Upon lifting the carpet, Frank noticed it was mostly dry, despite rain that had been intermittently falling throughout the night. Further examining the carpet, LaSota saw a large dark red, almost brown,

Top: Blood-covered plastic bag, Corey Slope. *Lackawanna County District Attorney.*

Bottom: Children's shoes, Corey Slope. *Lackawanna County District Attorney.*

bloodstain in the carpet's center, still wet, along with scrapings of what appeared to be a white, fleshy substance.

Recoiling, Frank LaSota yelled for his wife to look. Diane started walking toward her husband but then spotted a plastic newspaper carrier–type bag nearby covered by what seemed to be blood and a white fleshy substance. Frank LaSota began to dig around in the leaves, finding first a stick covered with blood and then a pile of what appeared to be made up of bones, hair and a gray/white type of material Frank thought to be pieces of brains. Frank LaSota stayed at the site while Diane ran down to find the police. Diane LaSota found firefighters Rich Rishko and Lou Materazzi at the end of the dirt road and told them of the couple's discovery up on Corey Slope.

Firefighter Lou Materazzi ran to an Old Forge police patrol car parked outside the Ziemba residence, alerting both Sergeant Biaranccardi and Patrolman Kelosky of the finding of bloody piece of carpet on Corey Slope. The police officers and the LaSotas further searched through the leaves on Corey Slope and found more bits of bone and clumps of hair.

Sergeant Biaranccardi uncovered what could only spell a sinister occurrence: a blood-soaked leather child's sandal. A blood-covered child's shower clog was also discovered. Old Forge Police Chief Lisowski arrived on Corey Slope, instructing the firefighters to rope off the area.

Trooper Kuklewicz and State Police Lieutenant Haschak arrived to assist securing the Corey Slope crime scene. The children's shoes, found on Corey Slope, were brought to be identified by the Ziemba family. Diane Ziemba was still awake, sitting with her friends and family on Doreen Propersi's front porch. A high-pitched scream emanated from Diane Ziemba and pierced the morning air of Connell's Patch. Shaking uncontrollably, Diane identified the sandals and shower clogs as having just been purchased for Cheryl and Christopher on Saturday's trip to New York. Diane Ziemba fell into a panic attack and was rushed to Moses Taylor Hospital.

State Police Lieutenant Mike Jordan was sitting at the breakfast table when the call came from State Police investigators on the ground in Old Forge confirming that Jordan's theory from the night before was now reality. Lieutenant Haschak twice repeated, "It looks like we have a double murder on our hands down here in Old Forge."

Jordan set out the instructions to Lieutenant Haschak necessary to begin an investigation. "Secure the crime scene, order the lab down to trailer park and have my unit come down from Dunmore….Finally, send for a helicopter to have Bill Rovinsky photograph the crime scene and above all else keep the press from the site."

THE DISTRICT ATTORNEY

S tosh had a bad feeling about the situation as he helped rope off the area at the top of Corey Slope. It was now known that the children's bloody footwear had been found.

Crowd control was now becoming a problem for the firefighters, as it seemed everyone in Old Forge was flocking to the base of Corey Slope. The police chief had pressed the firefighters into service to form a human chain around the site to keep out onlookers until reinforcements arrived from the State Police. The entire crowd wanted answers about what horror was found on Corey Slope.

Lackawanna County District Attorney Ernest "Ernie" Preate Jr., an Old Forge native, sat in his kitchen for an early morning breakfast prior to heading down to his office in Scranton. It had been a long day in politics attending a fundraiser clambake run by Doreen Propersi on Sunday, making this Monday morning seem more like the second, rather than the first, day of the workweek. Ernie Preate knew the Connell's Patch neighborhood well, having played many a baseball game on the ballfield adjacent to Corey Slope as a child.

Graduating from Old Forge High School in 1959, Preate graduated from the University of Pennsylvania and stayed on to earn a law degree in 1966. Preate became draft eligible for the Vietnam War following law school graduation. Rather than wait to be drafted into the army, Preate elected to join the U.S. Marine Corps. He served as an infantry platoon commander from 1968 to 1969 on the battlefields of Vietnam, clutching rosary beads his mother had given him.

Volunteer searchers receiving instructions, July 27, 1981. *From the* Scranton Times, *via the Lackawanna County Historical Society.*

Returning home in 1969, the young veteran began working for the family law firm and, to the chagrin of his father, immersed himself in the duties of being a part-time assistant district attorney. Ernie Preate soon spent much more time at his job at the District Attorney's Office rather than as an attorney at the law firm his father help found. Preate became a protégé to Lackawanna County District Attorney Paul Mazzoni, with his part-time position evolving into a full-time job as an assistant DA.

Preate proved his worth to Mazzoni assisting in the prosecution of the "Freach-Keen murders." On November 1, 1973, two junior high school students, Paul Freach and Edmond Keen, disappeared while walking home from school to their homes on Colliery Avenue in the Minooka section of Scranton. Four days later, their bodies were found under a piece of red carpet in a campground dump. Both boys had been sexually assaulted and shot in the head with a .25-caliber pistol.

This crime against young boys caused fear to grip the Scranton area like it had never felt before. The murders were so shocking that Mayor Eugene Peters, in the middle of a stiff campaign for reelection, ceased campaigning to direct all efforts at apprehending the killer of Paul Freach and Edmond Keen.

Excellent detective work by state trooper Gerald Gaetano and Scranton Police Detective Frank Karam led to the arrest of thirty-four-year-old William Wright. Wright was a previously convicted child murderer and paroled convict who was employed, on a work-release program, by a contractor hired by the City of Scranton for its rodent control program.

Paul Freach and Edmond Keen were within sight of their Colliery Avenue homes walking home from school when they were confronted by Wright brandishing a pistol. Wright molested the schoolboys and was holding them in his work van when a Scranton police officer knocked at the window wanting to know what he was doing parked on Colliery Avenue. The frightened boys did not make a sound, while Wright, in the driver's seat, convinced the questioning officer that he was parked on the street for legitimate purposes. After the police officer left the van, Wright killed both Paul Freach and Edmond Keen.

William Wright had a long criminal history and had previously been convicted in the 1960s of the murder of his own niece. Pennsylvania authorities had been aware, through Wright's own statements, of the murder of a four-year-old boy in Delaware County and of an adult female in Pittsburgh. Despite this knowledge of Wright's long criminal history, he was not prosecuted for the additional murders and was released on parole.

A hunch by state trooper Gerald Gaetano was instrumental in bringing Wright to justice. Genova theorized that the same individual who attempted to kidnap a hitchhiking college student at gunpoint the previous Friday and was responsible for the murders on Interstate 81 north of Scranton would be the killer of the teens. The college student, Thomas Nasser, when shown pictures of possible suspects, was immediately able to focus on William Wright's picture as the man who had attempted to kidnap him.

Following his arrest on December 19, 1973, and confronted by the weight of the evidence, William Wright originally pleaded guilty to the murders. Wright later changed his mind and changed his plea to not guilty. Public outrage was demonstrated by throngs of angry residents at Wright's preliminary hearing of December 28, 1973. Public defender John Dunn successfully petitioned for a change of venue of the trial to Bellefonte in Centre County, Pennsylvania, to ensure a fair trial. Rather than have William Wright face a jury, John Dunn elected to waive a jury trial and had his client's fate entrusted to Centre County Judge R. Paul Campbell in a bench trial, meaning the judge alone would determine the guilt or innocence of Wright.

Ernie Preate assisted District Attorney Paul Mazzoni throughout the trial of William Wright, expertly examining and cross-examining psychiatric experts regarding the sanity of Wright. The trial of William Wright was haunted by the daily presence of the parents of the slain boys, Ed and Dorothy Keen along with Paul and Gail Freach. Both Mazzoni and Ernie Preate attended the boys' funerals and vowed to the heartbroken parents to bring the killer of their children to justice. The promise of bringing the Freach-Keen killer to justice was kept at the murder trial, which began in September 1974 and resulted in his conviction on December 12. Wright was sentenced on April 24, 1975, to serve two consecutive life terms in prison. Given Wright's notoriety as a child molester and killer, he served his time in the Western Penitentiary in Pittsburgh, farther away from inmates from the eastern portion of the Commonwealth who would have a better chance of knowing of his past.

In May 1974, a baseball field on Colliery Avenue in Minooka was dedicated to the memory of Paul Freach and Edmond Keen. In 1975, both the Freach and the Kean families filed suit against the Pennsylvania Department of Correction, which allowed William Wright work-release parole with few restrictions.

Ernie Preate turned out to be a natural politician. When District Attorney Paul Mazzoni decided not to run for reelection in 1977, the Lackawanna County Republican Party organization, anxious to hold on to the office, turned to Ernie Preate as a candidate. Preate won the election by being portrayed as a tough, no-nonsense prosecutor who would never offer plea bargains for serious crimes.

As district attorney, Ernie Preate proved to be a deadly adversary to criminal defendants, obtaining a conviction in each case he brought to trial. Two talented assistant district attorneys, Larry Moran and newly hired Michael Barasse, regularly assisted Preate during trial, creating a devastatingly effective prosecution team.

In 1978, the Commonwealth of Pennsylvania reinstated the death penalty, calling for the imposition of a death sentence for offenders who committed first-degree murder when aggravating factors, such as kidnapping or multiple murders, were an element of the crime.

The first trial under Pennsylvania's new death penalty law was held in Lackawanna County, with Ernie Preate representing the Commonwealth. Abington Heights High School biology teacher Nicholas Karbin Jr. had come up with a diabolical plan to murder his estranged wife and deflect the attention of the police from him as a suspect. Karbin reasoned that a series of seemingly random murders would make the authorities think that a mad killer was on the loose. Then Karbin would kill his wife, hoping that her murder would be seen by the police to be just another victim of a serial killer.

The first confirmed victim of Karbin's scheme was James Shipman, shot and killed on a West Scranton Street in February 1978. Not satisfied with a single murder to create an impression that a serial killer was on the loose, Karbin, donning a fake beard, phony nose and glasses, came upon Gerald Walsh on North Main Avenue in Scranton, murdering him on March 17, 1978.

Two murders did not seem enough for Karbin's plot either, so on April 6, 1978, he went out in disguise looking again for random victims. This proved to be Karbin's undoing. Robert Christano was shot on a West Scranton Street, survived the attack and was able to identify his assailant. Karbin's school-age girlfriend, Lilith Howell, was angry that Karbin did not keep his promise to marry her and agreed to testify against him. Preate prosecuted Karbin for the two murders, which resulted in a conviction in February 1979. Since Pennsylvania's then new death penalty law had not been in effect at the time of the 1978 murders, Karbin received two consecutive life sentences.

Two murders did not satisfy Nicholas Karbin, who then proved he could commit murder while incarcerated. Clarence Doolittle was an illiterate, homeless vagrant who ended up living around the railroad yards in Scranton. Doolittle got into a fight with a fellow homeless vagrant, killing the man. Doolittle claimed self-defense as he awaited trial in the Lackawanna County Jail. Unfortunately for Clarence Doolittle, Nicholas Karbin was also a resident of the jail while he was awaiting sentencing for his 1978 murder spree.

One night in February 1979, the bigoted Karbin decided to dispense with the formality of a trial for Doolittle, who was African American. Karbin, along with other inmates wearing bedsheets as robes, put Clarence Doolittle on trial for murder. Karbin and the inmate jurists found Doolittle guilty of murder and hanged him with bedsheets.

Karbin's brutality against Clarence Doolittle bought him another murder trial, with Ernie Preate seeking the death penalty for the first time in Pennsylvania under the newly enacted death penalty law. The new murder charge against Nicholas Karbin made national news because of the murder's racial nature in what amounted to a lynching.

After the guilty verdict against Karbin on August 8, 1979, Ernie Preate skillfully argued to the jury for the death penalty during the sentencing phase of the trial. The jury unanimously condemned Karbin to die in the electric chair, making him the first resident of Pennsylvania's newly constituted death row.

The work ethic of Ernest Preate Jr. had always been, "Be at work early and do not pass work to an assistant that should be done by oneself." When the phone rang at 7:00 a.m. on Monday morning, July 27, 1981, Ernie Preate was already preparing for a day at the office. The call was hardly good news. Lieutenant Michael Jordan of the Pennsylvania State Police noted that everything in Old Forge indicated that the Ziemba children had been murdered. Preate was quick to call Assistant District Attorney Larry Moran, instructing him to be in Old Forge in thirty minutes to coordinate the efforts of the District Attorney's Office with those of the State Police.

INVESTIGATIVE TEAM

The greatest skill Lieutenant Mike Jordan possessed as an investigator was his ability to organize subordinates into a well-rounded investigative team. It was now of prime importance that Jordan organize his forces to investigate the crime scene on Corey Slope.

Trooper William Rovinsky was ordered to photograph the crime scene by helicopter. A helicopter landed in the ballfield at the north end of Corey Slope and lifted Rovinsky with his camera in tow to the skies above the neighborhood.

Trooper Walter Carlson arrived at Corey Slope at 7:30 a.m. to examine what had been found by volunteer searchers. Climbing the dirt road up the Corey Slope, Carlson discovered a group of searchers debating the discovery made by the LaSotas. Examining the grisly discovery, Carlson put to rest the arguments regarding the substance that covered the leaves and carpet pieces, identifying what was found to be human remains.

The discovery of blood-covered sandals and a shower clog further confirmed Carlson's belief that the Ziemba children had been murdered. It was apparent to Carlson that the kids had not been murdered at this site, but rather that some of the debris of the crime had been disposed of on Corey Slope.

The obscure location of Corey Slope led Carlson to conclude that this crime was not the work of someone from outside this neighborhood. "Nobody outside this neighborhood would know this place even exists so we will have to keep an eye on this area," Carlson said to his partner, Bob James.

After supervising the roping off of the crime scene, Carlson and James climbed down Corey Slope onto Hard Street and walked down toward the Ziemba home. During their hike from Corey Slope, the troopers noticed a house on Hard Street between Seaman Lane and Olivia Street. The house, a white and brown two-story, did not seem complete. A door to the outside on the second floor stood forlorn, without stairs to the ground below. A front door stood boarded up, while the garage door was missing windows, replaced by hurricane fence material.

In the driveway of the home stood a small white car, up on jacks, which appeared to be in the process of being worked on by someone. "What ya looking for?" came a voice from the side of the house as a thin teenager with thick glasses approached. "We're state troopers…has this house been searched for the kids?" Carlson replied. "Yes, it was checked last night and locked up," the boy responded.

The teenager informed the troopers that his name was Joey Aulisio and continued to make small talk with Carlson and James until they left the property. "That kid had a real bug up his ass the way he followed us around his property," Carlson commented to his partner.

Mike Jordan firmly believed that superb organization made for an effective investigative team and set about to rapidly organize his command. It was always of prime importance to create two-man investigative units whose personalities complemented each other. Mike Jordan considered one member of each two-man team to be an "investigative killer," a relentless investigator driven by a desire to take whatever action necessary to solve the case.

Complementing the skills of the "investigative killer" stood a trooper who played a more passive role of measuring the inquiry of his partner against other clues unearthed. Gerald "Pete" Gaetano was one such "investigative killer," who when combined with his partner, Trooper Billy Padula, made for an effective team. Walter Carlson and Bob James were another important pair of investigators at Mike Jordan's disposal.

Nick Genova, who had been instrumental in cracking the Freach-Keen murder case, also arrived at the command post to join the investigation. Now forces were assembled so Jordan could set about deploying his detectives. An immediate problem confronting the investigation was that onlookers were now surrounding the crime scene, driven by reports on television regarding Corey Slope. Dozens of extra state troopers had been called to the scene to assist with crowd control.

The heavy State Police presence in Old Forge led all but the most naïve of the press corps to believe that there was a lot more to the disappearance of the Ziemba children than the authorities would admit. Jordan's reply to the questions of the media was simply that "the State Police are only assisting in a missing children investigation."

Kitch Loftus, a local radio reporter of 590 WARM Radio, known to listeners around the Scranton area as the "News Girl," followed Jordan as he made his way to the on-site command post. "Don't you lie to me, Mike Jordan," Loftus shouted. "You and your detectives don't look for lost children, that isn't your job—your job is about murder." Jordan momentarily stared back at Loftus, wondering whether the reporter knew just how correct she was.

Mike Jordan had already set up operations of the "crime scene command post" in the Propersi kitchen when Troopers Carlson and James checked in for further instructions. Bill Rovinsky and other members of the evidence and records team were already airborne, taking aerial photos of the Corey Slope area. Jordan laid out on the kitchen table the debris that had been found up on Corey Slope to be tagged for identification by the mobile State Police Crime Lab. An old piece of blue carpet that was stained with blood dominated the scene.

The searchers found the carpet that morning, and only its ends were damp. "Since it rained throughout the night, this entire rug would have been soaked had it been out there all night," Jordan commented. "I'd like to follow this carpet as a lead and see where it takes us," Trooper Genova said, adding, "I think this thing is going to be key."

"What's the line on the parents?" Carlson asked, knowing through experience that parents and relatives were always the first suspects to be checked out in such an investigation. "The mother fainted when she saw the shoes, and her husband took her over to Moses Taylor Hospital," Jordan replied as he looked over to the three sandals found on Corey Slope. Two leather Dr. Scholl's sandals, covered with blood, identified as belonging to Cheryl Ziemba, had been recovered, along with a rubber shower clog Christopher was last reported to have been wearing. The children-sized shoes found up on Corey Slope had a haunting presence to them, as only a day before living, breathing kids had been wearing them.

Sometimes to catch a killer, it takes the mind of a killer. That's what Mike Jordan thought as he picked up the telephone to call into the State Police Barracks. Jordan knew that one of the best sources of information regarding the criminal mind was found in the prisons of Pennsylvania.

As a general policy, prison inmates from Lackawanna County were incarcerated at Graterford Prison outside Philadelphia; however, high-profile prisoners in danger of attack were often imprisoned at facilities where they would be less well known. Child killers are held in low esteem in prison society and often subject to attack by other inmates.

William Wright had been placed in segregated custody at the Western Penitentiary near Pittsburgh since having been sentenced to life imprisonment in 1975 for the murders of Paul Freach and Edmond Keen. Wright was fortunate that there were few inmates from the Scranton area in the prison populace who would have a more complete knowledge of his crimes. The greatest threat to Wright was the prospect of being transferred to the prison's general population.

A state trooper stood in the Western Penitentiary of Pennsylvania visiting room, awaiting a meeting with inmate William Wright. If there was one man who knew the mind of a child killer, it was Wright.

The trooper recoiled at the sight of the prisoner, as it was difficult not to despise the man who entered the room. The inmate still bore the features exhibited on the front page of the *Scranton Times* eight years before. The trooper passed to Wright a small file that contained a basic outline of the Ziemba investigation. The prisoner gazed with an icy stare at the pages, which revealed the discoveries made on Corey Slope along with the descriptions of the neighborhood.

"Corey Slope would not be known by anybody except from the immediate neighborhood—look for someone local," Wright said, not bothering to look up from the file. "It takes a lot of trust to snatch a kid, so look for somebody they know." Now staring at the trooper, the killer blurted out his final words of the conversation: "Don't limit yourselves to looking at just adults on this one—look to local teenagers, specifically a male."

PRESS CONFERENCE

S omething must have happened to Diane's kids—why else would Preate be here?" yelled an elderly woman from the crowd of onlookers as the district attorney arrived at Corey Slope. The younger women with children, scattered throughout the crowd, seemed to recoil and instinctively pulled their progeny closer as though to shield them from an evil curse. Grimly surveying Corey Slope and ignoring the sunlight's glare from the slate-strewn hill, Preate turned to Larry Moran and said, "I want a shoulder-to-shoulder search conducted of Corey Slope and the surrounding woods."

"My God, Mike, this looks like Freach-Keen all over again," Preate said to Jordan after viewing the evidence recovered. "From what I've been told so far, we can rule out the parents of the kids," Preate said. "Their story is consistent, and their reaction to what has happened speaks for itself—we've had investigators interview just about everybody who knows the Ziembas, so we have a pretty good picture of the home life," Jordan responded. "My guys are not quick to jump to conclusions when judging the reaction of victims' families—we had a case out in East Stroudsburg last year where a few of my guys were sure this lady's husband killed her because he showed no emotion when told his wife was dead," Mike Jordan continued. Shaking his head at the insanity of it all, Jordan added, "It turned out the guy's girlfriend murdered the wife without his knowledge—we caught her because she left a piece of her broken nail at the crime scene."

"That whole investigation taught the troopers of this unit not to be quick to judge just on somebody's reaction," Jordan concluded. "A lot of people didn't like how Diane Ziemba was acting last night just sitting on her porch crying while the whole town was out looking for her kids, but when you look at it in context, fear has a way of paralyzing a person into inaction....We can rule out Diane and Chester Ziemba as suspects from this point onward."

The carpets recovered on Corey Slope were stained in blood with hairs and fragments of human flesh. "Christ, whoever did this must have dismembered these kids—let's order a stop to garbage collection and have the searchers check the sewers in Old Forge," Preate said to Mike Jordan with an audible strain in his voice. Preate knew that the horror of the Freach-Keen murders had indeed repeated. To leave the question of who murdered the Ziemba children unanswered for any length of time was unsatisfactory.

The rumors fueled by the reports from searchers soon reached a fever pitch, having been disseminated throughout Lackawanna County by the media. It was obvious to Preate that a press conference was necessary to stem the panic enveloping the public. The press was summoned to the White-Eagle Hose Firehouse, which was soon inundated with members of the media, searchers and the curious.

Silence was maintained by the gathered multitude as Preate walked up to a microphone to address the press. "We have found no body or bodies, but what we did find gives us cause for grave concern," Preate told the tense gathering. He then spoke of the gruesome discoveries: "At the top of a secluded slate hill, under some bushes and trees we found three bloodstained shoes that have been tentatively identified as belonging to the Ziemba children. Nearby were found some fragments of what appeared to be bone, flesh, hair and brain, enough to fit into one hand. The discovery was made by one of the volunteer searchers earlier in the morning, but we chose not to say anything about it until after laboratory tests confirmed it was what we feared it to be."

The crowd stood dumbfounded by Preate's revelations. He continued to relay more information regarding the gruesome discoveries: "Near the shoes the searchers found two sections of carpet—one dark blue and the other white shag—they were both covered with blood and flesh. Foul play is suspected, and as of this moment, my office along with the state and local police will treat this matter as a double homicide. We have no suspects at this point, nor are we sure what type of weapon could have been used to produce the kind of findings uncovered. Ballistics tests—"

Preate stopped momentarily as he realized that he was revealing publicly more than he wanted known. Correcting himself, he continued, "We don't have any proof if firearms figure into this case, and more laboratory tests

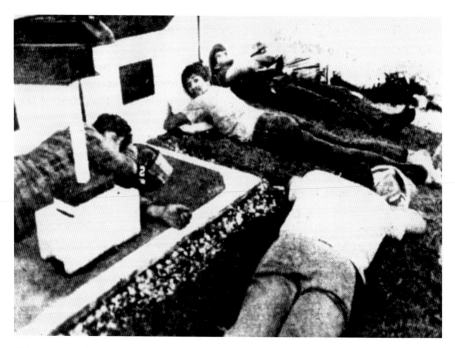

Volunteer searchers rest, July 27, 1981. *From the* Scranton Times, *via the Lackawanna County Historical Society.*

are needed. Right now, we are looking for leads, and I appeal to anyone with information that might be helpful to please, please come forward. All information will be treated in strict confidence, and the police are especially interested in knowing whether anyone had seen strange people or strange cars in the neighborhood or anyone carrying carpet in the vicinity of the culm bank."

"It looks bad," Preate muttered to himself out loud. Shocked by his own inability to keep his thoughts to himself, Preate turned to Ray Jeffries, the maternal grandfather of Cheryl and Christopher, standing near the front of the assembled crowd, and said, "I'm sorry."

Preate continued, "We're going to shake the trees until somebody falls out—this must be the work of a deviant." When pressed as to what motive could there be to murder young children, Preate answered with a rhetorical question. "What other motive could it be? It certainly wasn't robbery; it could be just a case of someone who likes little boys—the case reminds me a lot of the Freach-Keen murders." Preate then alluded to a possible connection with the neighborhood: "Most every neighborhood has its share of weird people, and we hope to locate them here whether or not they have a criminal record. The office of the district attorney has ordered trash collection in Old Forge be suspended until further notice, and we have sent officers to search the landfill through the trash that had already been collected this morning."

Reporter Bill Haplan asked Jordan how many troopers the State Police would assign to the investigation. Jordan responded, "There are 4,000 troopers in the Pennsylvania State Police, and as many of those as it takes will be assigned."

Upon the conclusion of the press conference, Stosh and his companions returned to conduct another shoulder-to-shoulder search of the woods beyond Corey Slope. "Preate must know that there is something up in these woods," Mike Nalevanko said to Stosh as the pair prepared to scale Corey Slope. "We've been up here at least a dozen times already," Mike continued. Stosh turned to Mike as they began searching the woods and said, "I sure don't want to be the one to find the bodies of little kids."

The early afternoon heat and fatigue were taking a toll on the volunteer searchers, who upon exiting the woods collapsed on the baseball field adjacent to Corey Slope. Two state troopers approached Stosh and Mike asking if anyone knew anything about the sewer system of Old Forge. "The system is built into the old mine shafts under the town, as are the septic systems of most people," Mike replied. "If anything gets thrown down there, it could end up several hundred feet underground," Stosh added.

Night was beginning to descend, with no further clues discovered regarding the Ziemba children. Sergeant Biaranccardi drove down Connell Street to check the area down by Deater's Lane before it got dark. He had considered driving up the road that led up the mountains but decided that the rocky trail would damage the car's undercarriage. Just before he exited the dirt road, he spied a blanket sitting in the weeds.

Normally, Biaranccardi would have just driven right by the blanket, but for some reason, it did not seem right that such an object was lying in the weeds on the deserted road. The very isolation of the location made him suspicious of anything unusual along the road. Very few vehicles normally traversed this dirt road, which led to old strip mining pits.

The road that led up the mountain dated from the days when trucks brought mineral wealth down from the now abandoned stripping pits perched above the town. The Popple Brothers property itself stretched from the end of Connell Street to the banks of the Lackawanna River.

Biaranccardi froze as he examined his discovery. The beige blanket with horse and Indian designs was covered from top to bottom with what could only be dried blood. He jumped back into his patrol car and raced up to the command post on Drakes Lane. Trooper Nicky Genova was on duty in the Propersi kitchen when Biaranccardi brought in his discovery. Trooper Genova contacted Jordan by radio to come back to the command post immediately. Genova took care not to reveal anything over the airways since in all probability the press was monitoring transmissions over scanners.

"Let's get this to Bill Rovinsky right away," Mike Jordan ordered. Trooper Rovinsky, the evidence officer, after performing initial tests in the Mobile State Police Crime Lab, tagged and forwarded the evidence to the State Police lab at the Wyoming, Pennsylvania barracks. In a few hours, the lab confirmed that the stains on the blanket were human blood.

Mike Jordan was walking with Corporal Lavatt to the on-site command post from Corey Slope when a volunteer searcher ran up to the pair stating that he had found what appeared to be a blood-covered blanket in an old washing machine in a nearby yard. Jordan and Lavatt followed the searcher onto the property and scanned the area with flashlights.

Jordan viewing the property, noting that it consisted of a trailer home and a semi-finished home on the Hard Street side of the yard facing the baseball field, with Corey Slope about one hundred feet to the west. Between the brown trailer home and the house were grapevines and a log hut. An old pickup truck was parked at the rear of the house, and the washing machine in question stood opposite the aged vehicle. Shining flashlights into the washing machine, Jordan and Lavatt saw an old blanket with some streaks of red paint.

"What are you doing on my property?" came a voice from behind Jordan. "I'm Lieutenant Jordan of the State Police, and this is Corporal Lavatt—we're investigating a report of evidence on this property," Jordan responded, adding the question, "Who are you?" to the skinny kid with thick glasses who had issued the challenge.

The youth replied, "I'm Joey Aulisio, and my father owns this property. Right now, we live in the trailer, but as soon as the electricity is hooked up, my dad, brother and me are going to move into this house." "Has this house been searched?" Jordan inquired. "My father, brother and me searched the house, and it's been locked up all day to keep people from stealing anything out of it," the teenager responded. Satisfied with the boy's answers, Jordan left the Aulisio yard and returned to the command post.

TUESDAY MORNING

Tuesday began with a meeting for all searchers at the White-Eagle Hose Firehouse, where instructions were given regarding the focus of the day's search. Stosh Zoltewicz, along with his fellow firefighters, decided to search for the Ziemba children as a team, adding Rich Besancon of White-Eagle Hose to their search party. While all hope was gone for finding Chris and Cheryl alive, the men believed that retrieving the remains would at least allow for a decent burial.

Preate and the State Police were directing the search parties to concentrate on searching for any sign of the kids within Old Forge itself, as the Corey Slope area had been thoroughly searched. Several of the volunteers were sent to sift through ashes and debris at the area landfill. Preate ordered an intense search of the Old Forge sewer system and septic tanks. The banks of the Lackawanna River were to be thoroughly inspected.

Stosh and Ed concluded that the bodies of Cheryl and Christopher must be somewhere other than where the search had been concentrated. The news of a blanket having been found up on Deater's Lane gave rise among the group to a rhetorical question: "Where in Old Forge could one hide a body?" By any standard, the old strip mining pits above Deater's Lane up in Connell's Patch formed the most isolated and least visited section of town.

Stosh told the trooper in charge of coordinating the searchers that his group was going to conduct a search of the mining pits. The trooper said, "I can't stop you, so do what you want to do, but there's no way anything could be up that far." The group decided to head up the mountain in Ed's Blazer. The hot summer air churned through the open windows of the vehicle, heading onto the dirt road up the mountain.

Searching the stripping pits atop the mountain turned out to be uneventful. Stosh and Frank Genell explored the perimeter of one pit while Mike, Ed and Rich investigated the other. Having found nothing in either stripping pit, the group decided to head down the mountain and check the next such crater on the way back down to Old Forge.

Working according to plan, Stosh and Frank checked the next stripping pit closest to Old Forge, with the remainder of the firefighters searching the other pit across the road nearest Duryea. Stosh yelled over to Frank to follow him down to the bottom of the stripping pit to investigate the hulks of some rusting automobiles.

Frank had made it about thirty feet down from the edge of the pit when he caught a glimpse of something that stopped him in his tracks. Genell focused his eyes on a red cloth a few feet below him and noticed a little leg sticking out from beneath a piece of blue carpet. Another pair of legs stuck out from underneath a white piece of carpet as flies swarmed around the area. Genell covered his face and yelled, "Stosh! Stosh! Stosh!"

Zoltewicz knew when he heard Frank's screams that the bodies of the Ziemba children had been found. Stosh ran over to Frank, who was "white as a shirt," pointing toward the bottom of the stripping pit. Stosh saw the bodies of the Ziemba children partially covered by carpets, snapping his head quickly away. The other men turned to one another at the sound of Genell's screams, and all knew instinctively that Frank had located the bodies. Genell sat on the ground with his head between his legs as the rest of the men rushed over to the edge of the strip mining pit. Once Frank had regained his breath, all five men stood at the edge of the stripping and looked over to confirm what had been found.

The bodies of the Ziemba children "did not look right," reminding Mike of mannequins. Ed's first thought was that he and his fellow firefighters had done their job finding the kids and that was it. The one clear thing was that the firefighters would have to get the State Police up to the stripping pit on the double. "Stosh, you, Frank and Rich stay up here and secure the area, and we'll take the truck and get the troopers," Ed instructed.

Ed's Blazer bumped along the dirt road, traveling at speeds that he would never have dreamed of on such a road. Ed turned to Mike with a look of worry on his face and said, "We left them back up there. What if the killer is still up there?"

Aerial view of the strip mine location. *From the* Scranton Times-Tribune, *via the Lackawanna County Historical Society.*

An eerie silence enveloped the strip mining pit as the tail lights of Ed's Blazer disappeared down the mountain road. Frank did not look so good, and Stosh did not feel well either in the morning heat. "Let's get off the road and stand off in the shade of the woods," Stosh said. Stosh did not want to make Frank more nervous than he already was, but the possibility existed that whoever did this to the children was perhaps still up on the mountain watching them. The wait for help was nerve-wracking. Overhead, a television news helicopter began to circle in the sky above the stripping pit. Just when Frank, Rich and Stosh thought they could not be more scared, out from the woods came walking toward them a bare-chested man wearing army fatigue pants and holding a machete in his right hand. Stosh could not help uttering, "I think this is it guys."

Ed raced his truck onto Connell Street, where Old Forge Police Chief Lisowski happened to be sitting in a patrol car. Pulling up to the chief's car, Ed yelled out the window, "We found the kids' bodies up on the mountain, and we left three men up there to secure the area." "Go tell the troopers at White-Eagle, and I'll start blocking off the road," Chief Lisowski yelled back to Ed.

Ed drove to White-Eagle Hose, where most of the state troopers were taking a breakfast break. The troopers' bacon and eggs were interrupted by Ed and Mike storming into the firehouse with the news—"We found the kids' bodies up on the mountain, and three of our friends are up there alone with them." Troopers sprang into action upon hearing this, with several piling into Ed's Blazer followed by several carloads of troopers traveling up the mountain road. Old Forge police blocked off Deater's Lane from Connell Street, while volunteer firefighters formed a human chain in the woods to prevent onlookers from going up the mountain. The fury of activity drove many people to the edge of Connell Street, as they seemed to be able to sense that something was radically wrong up on the mountain.

Stosh chose a large rock and prepared to defend himself, Rich and Frank as best he could. It was a challenge that did not have to be met, as Ed pulled up in his Blazer followed by about a dozen State Police cars. State troopers, with guns drawn, surrounded the man with the machete, quickly disarming him. "You had us scared shitless," Mike said to Stosh. Stosh shouted back, "You think you were scared shitless? Imagine how we felt about it." The area was now covered with state troopers, with some questioning the guy with the machete and others attempting to make their way down the slope to the bodies of Christopher and Cheryl.

Mike Jordan peered over the edge of the striping pit and observed the bloody pile of debris that contained the bodies of Cheryl and Christopher. The steep bank of the abandoned mine pit made it necessary to utilize ropes for troopers to be lowered to the actual location of the bodies, which was about thirty feet from the roadside. It appeared that the children were thrown from the edge of the pit and rolled downward until hitting a tree. A piece of dark-blue carpeting had been thrown on top of the children, along with a blood-covered white shag rug.

A television news helicopter was now hovering directly overhead. Mike Jordan considered the prospect of the bodies of the Ziemba children being televised on live TV. Jordan radioed to the command post to have a message relayed to the helicopter crew: "Tell them if they do not get out of here, I will shoot down that bird." The helicopter hovered for a minute, its crew taking in Jordan's relayed message, when Jordan unholstered his sidearm in full view of the aircraft. Looking down at Jordan, the crew of the helicopter quickly left the crime scene, flying off to the east.

The body of Cheryl Lynn Ziemba lay at a side angle about ten feet away from the corpse of her brother. A length of red electrical wire lay atop Christopher Ziemba, as though the killer decided to discard his unwanted garbage along with the bodies of his victims.

It seemed clear to Mike Jordan that the assailant must have had an intimate knowledge of the area since it could not have been mere chance

Portion of Mine Road where bodies were dumped. *Lackawanna County District Attorney.*

that the children were removed to this isolated location by someone who was a stranger to Old Forge. It was also clear that whoever murdered the children had made a mistake that would provide the means of tracking him down. A trooper had recovered and brought up to the road for examination a piece of white shag carpet cut in the shape of an automobile dashboard. Looking carefully at the carpet, Jordan muttered, "Whoever it is made a big mistake here. We've got him—it's just a matter of time."

Top: White shag carpet cut out for a dashboard. *Lackawanna County District Attorney.*

Bottom: Blue carpet found with bodies. *Lackawanna County District Attorney.*

Opposite: Venetian blind with a tire mark. *Lackawanna County District Attorney.*

The white shag carpet was handed to Trooper Rovinsky, who noted that the back was coated with what appeared to be dried glue. "This had to have been attached to a dashboard, so if we find the car this goes to, we can find the killer....I'll make a tinplate from this and bring it down to the DeNaples junkyard to see if we can match this up." Helicopter photos of the crime scene were ordered before the children's bodies could be removed from the slope of the pit.

The examination by William Sweeney, the coroner of Lackawanna County, of the remains found up on Corey Slope revealed in the brain matter and hair several 12-gauge shotgun pellets and a plastic shotgun shell wad. Mike Jordan now theorized that the children were killed in one location, with pieces of their remains left up on Corey Slope.

Whoever the killer was left enough clues that could be pieced together and tracked. At the top of the pit, a car had been backed up, leaving an imprint of a tire on a piece of a discarded venetian blind. A cast of the tire imprint was taken, and the piece of blind was placed into an evidence bag. While the photographs were being taken by helicopter, troopers searched

Ziemba children's bodies arrive at Scranton State Hospital. *From the* Scranton Times, *via the Lackawanna County Historical Society.*

the ground near the bodies for any further clues. After the photos of the area were completed, troopers brought the bodies up from the pit with ropes and pulleys.

Dr. Dominic DiMaio, a retired New York City medical examiner, had been requested to travel to Scranton by Preate to conduct the autopsies of Cheryl and Christopher. Jordan ordered the troopers under his command to the on-site command post for a strategy meeting prior to a press conference scheduled by Ernie Preate.

After questioning, the shirtless man with the machete was discounted as having any connection with the murders. Ernie Preate arrived at the crime scene, and all could see the look of disgust on his face. "We'll do whatever it takes to get this guy," Mike Jordan said. "This is not going to be a pretty press conference," Preate responded.

The crowd at White-Eagle Hose seemed to expect the worst when they assembled for the press conference. In a soft, regretful voice, Preate told the crowd, "What we have feared has come to pass." A silence hung over the bays of the firehouse as a woman quieted an infant in her arms. "Firemen recovered the bodies of the Ziemba children thirty feet off a dirt road in an abandoned strip mine."

Left: Ernest D. Preate Jr. at the press conference. *From the* Scranton Times-Tribune, *via the Lackawanna County Historical Society.*

Below: Searchers who discovered bodies. *From the* Wilkes-Barre Times-Leader.

"Chris received a gunshot wound to the chest," Preate uttered. The crowd gasped as though the wind had been knocked out of them. A slight cough came from Preate, who then added, "Cheryl received a gunshot wound to the head." A moan of disbelief came from the crowd. "The intensive search will continue until the murderer has been apprehended," Preate said, concluding the press conference.

The horror of the Freach-Keen case was now being relived for Lackawanna County residents. Old Forge Bank was offering a $1,000 reward for information leading to the apprehension of whoever was responsible for this crime. Danny Salamone, the owner of the World-Wide Flag Company, was offering a similar reward. The headline being prepared for the *Scranton Times* stated, "Help Catch a Killer," imploring anyone with information to come forward.

Ed summed up his group of firefighters' feelings best, stating to the reporters, "You can't be proud of finding what we did; you're proud when you go into a burning building and pull a child out to safety—this is nothing to be proud of."

Ideally, Stosh and his friends wanted to remain unidentified, as the killer was still out there. Preate assured the group that their names would not be revealed to the press. No sooner had that promise been made than Preate came walking up to them with reporters in tow, saying, "These are the firemen who found the bodies up on the mountain." "Thanks a lot, Ernie," Stosh, Ed and Mike said in unison. "Now everybody knows who we are." Frank was so shaken up that he had gone home to calm down.

SUFFER LITTLE CHILDREN

Troopers Merenich, Rovinsky and Morgan stared down the embankment at Cheryl and Christopher Ziemba. The little girl was lying on her back about thirty-one feet north of the dirt road. She was clothed in a red tank top and red shorts. A pair of size 28–29 Wrangler blue jeans were tied around the girl's head.

Christopher Ziemba lay on his right side ten feet away from his sister. A red and blue blanket had been thrown over the child that, when removed, revealed a small entry wound in the upper right chest of what appeared to be a Superman T-shirt. A piece of black electrical wire with three connectors attached rested atop the little boy, and another piece of wire was found ten feet to the south between the body and the road.

Trooper Morgan headed to the Wyoming barracks to make a tinplate of the piece of white shag carpet that had been cut in the shape of an auto dashboard. Troopers Rovinsky and Merenich accompanied the bodies of Cheryl and Christopher to Scranton State Hospital for autopsy.

Upon arrival at the hospital, the troopers and the Lackawanna County coroner were met by a swarm of press, led by Joseph Silva, the general manager of radio stations WEJL and WEZX. Inside the hospital, Dr. Dominic DiMaio performed the autopsy.

DiMaio had been a forensic pathologist since 1940. He had been with the Office of the Medical Examiner of New York City for a period of thirty years, retiring as chief examiner in 1978. During his career, DiMaio had performed more than twenty thousand autopsies. At age sixty-nine, Dr. DiMaio was still actively participating in his field.

Former New York Medical Examiner Dr. Dominic DiMaio. *From the* Scranton Times, *via the Lackawanna County Historical Society.*

Television reporter Frank Andrews stood silently with newspaper reporter Joseph Flaherty of the *Scranton Times*, watching the arrival of the bodies at a respectful distance. Flaherty thought of his own children as the body bags were removed from the hearse. A lump filled Flaherty's throat as he watched the little bodies being carried dutifully by state troopers into the hospital—the scene brought back painful memories of his coverage of the Freach-Keen murders.

DiMaio first performed the autopsy of Cheryl Lynn Ziemba, assisted by Coroner Tom Sweeny as Trooper Rovinsky looked on. A pair of loose size-28 blue jeans were tied around the head of Cheryl that, when removed, revealed a gaping shotgun wound on the child's head. There was almost complete avulsion, meaning Cheryl's skull was literally torn apart.

Utilizing the bone fragments found up on Corey Slope, DiMaio was able to reconstruct Cheryl's head except for a ⅛-inch-diameter hole that marked the entrance wound of a shotgun blast. Through this wound, innumerable pellets were directed in a downward path imbedded in the base of the child's skull.

Blue and silver fragments of glass were found imbedded in Cheryl's skull along with shotgun pellets, all of which were collected and turned over to Trooper Rovinsky as evidence. There were no obvious signs of sexual molestation, as had been expected in a case such as this.

The shotgun wound on Christopher was situated on the right-hand side of the child's chest, commonly known as the "mid-line" of the torso. Further examination revealed a shotgun perforation measured one inch in diameter, with an abrasion contusion on the edge of the wound. The path of the deadly shotgun pellets proceeded in a downward trajectory, passing through the right fifth and sixth ribs, tearing a laceration in the lower third of the victim's heart.

Death had been instantaneous for Christopher Ziemba, as it had been for his sister. Dr. DiMaio discovered the plastic wadding of a 12-gauge shotgun shell, the apparent source of the abrasion, near the entry wound. The fact that the shotgun wadding was found inside of Christopher indicated to DiMaio that the blast fired at the little boy was at extremely close range.

During the autopsies, Trooper Rovinsky collected and bagged as evidence the various discoveries made by Dr. DiMaio. Many of what were determined to be "number 6" shotgun pellets were recovered from the children, along with the small pieces of metallic glass that had been removed from Cheryl.

Strands of hair were removed from Cheryl, and fingernail scrapings from each child were collected for examination by the State Police Lab. Upon conclusion of the autopsies, all evidence gathered was tagged and taken personally by Trooper Rovinsky to the Pennsylvania State Police Crime Lab. Following the examination of the evidence by State Police scientist George Surma, all items were to be sent to the FBI crime lab in Washington, D.C., for further analysis.

THE DISAPPEARANCE OF THE Ziemba children did not seem to concern Joey Aulisio. His priority was to fix the Cricket's oil pan. Joey had pounded out the oil pan with a hammer and poured gasoline into the pan thereafter to see if it leaked. Gasoline leaked all over the driveway, demonstrating that the oil pan would have to be welded or soldered.

J.R. Davis trudged over to the driveway to see what Joey was up to. J.R. asked Joey, "Hey, Joey, are you fixing your oil pan?" Aulisio just stared at his friend, annoyed to be asked such a stupid question. J.R.'s next question was much less stupid and seemed to require and actual answer: "Hey Joey, how did the oil pan break?" "I ran over a ramp in the yard," Aulisio replied.

Robert Colburn, Joey's best friend, strolled into the yard and watched Joey work on the oil pan. "Joey, what happened to the oil pan?" "A fireman came into the yard last night and put a hole in it with a screwdriver," Joey replied. Colburn examined the oil pan, which seemed to him creased with small pieces of rock embedded in the bottom. The whole thing seemed strange. It did not seem to Colburn like a screwdriver could have done this sort of damage.

Diane Ziemba looked up from her hospital bed to see Trooper Walter Carlson standing in the doorway. Carlson looked at Diane and Cookie and in a soft voice said, "We have found the children." Color and enthusiasm rushed into Diane's face as she looked toward the door, expecting Cheryl and Chris to come running into the room.

The color in Diane's face drained to an ashen white a moment later when she looked at the state trooper's face. Trooper Carlson said, "I am very sorry." Involuntary shaking began to contort the young mother's body as tears cascaded down her face and a silent scream wailed from her mouth. Tears burst from the eyes of Cookie Ziemba as his face shook with rage and anguish. Nursing staff, family and friends came into the room, attempting to console the couple as best they could. Trooper Carlson sadly withdrew from the room, wishing to inflict no more pain on the heartbroken couple. Carlson turned to Trooper James and motioned with his arm that they should leave.

A heavyset teenager confronted the troopers as they left the floor of the hospital. "What will happen to the guy who did this?" the teen asked. "Who are you?" Trooper Carlson responded. "Bobby Aulisio.…I came down here to see how Diane is doing." Since the kid was a neighbor and family friend, it was possible that he observed something everybody else missed, so Carlson decided to continue questioning the youth.

Bobby's responses were not what the trooper expected, as the kid seemed at once to be evasive to simple questions and yet inquisitive regarding the status of the police investigation. "What will happen to the guy who did this?" the youth asked. It all struck Carlson as strange that this kid was interested in what would happen to the killer.

It seemed no one would have a right to interrupt the privacy of Diane Ziemba, and there was not a soul that could say to the young mother, "I know how you feel." However, there was a mother who did know what it was like to stand in the shoes of Diane Ziemba. Gail Freach had felt the kind of pain Diane now had to endure when she had lost her young son Paul to murderer William Wright.

Gail Freach found herself at Diane Ziemba's bedside, helping her cope with feelings that few people could understand. Debbie Freach, a nurse on Diane Ziemba's floor, was the sister of murder victim Paul Freach. She had alerted her mother to Diane's presence on the floor, and together the two women attempted to ease the pain of a heartbroken mother.

The similarity of the case to the Freach-Keen murders provoked the attention of the local press, opening the old wounds suffered by the families of the murdered boys. Paul Freach, father of the youngster slain eight years before, reflected to Joseph X. Flannery, columnist for the *Scranton Times*, "I sympathize with them—it is a terrible thing to go through." Upon further reflection, Mr. Freach told Flannery that the loss the Ziembas had suffered was even greater than that of his own family: "They were their only children…we had our four daughters and the Keens had theirs…but now the Ziembas are alone.…That's—." Choked with emotion, Paul Freach could not finish his interview with the columnist.

For Cookie Ziemba, it was the end of his world as he knew it. He came home to the family's Drakes Lane apartment to find that what had once been filed with happiness now contained only heartbreak. He sadly packed his wife's bags, as they would be moving in with his parents, as neither he nor Diane could stand the memories of Drakes Lane. Diane Ziemba ultimately would never return to the neighborhood again.

In front of his apartment, Cookie Ziemba faced Mike Jordan, whose facial expression was at once sympathetic and yet determined. He told Cookie what had been found up on the mountain and expressed his condolences to the man whose heart had been crushed by the events of the past forty-eight hours.

Reporters stood near the two men, strangers just two days before, as the sun set above the mountains to the west. *Scranton Times* reporter Francis De Andrea observed Mr. Ziemba's eyes flood with tears, and the tears ran off the man's face onto the sidewalk. Clasping the grief-stricken father's hand, Jordan made a simple promise: "We will get who did this."

Bob Aulisio had arrived home from Doylestown after picking up his girlfriend, Phyllis, who had been house sitting. The thought that Joey may have had something to do with the kids' disappearance dominated Bob's thinking. Bob didn't know why his mind kept linking Joey to Cheryl and Christopher, tormenting him the entire ride back to Old Forge. "Maybe we can bring the boys out to Revello's for pizza when we get home and get them out of the neighborhood for a while," Bob said, turning to Phyllis. Upon arriving back in Old Forge, the pair was greeted with the news that the Ziemba kids had been found murdered up on the mountain.

"Franko," a frequent visitor of Lenny Brown's from New Jersey, had come by to see Lenny and Doreen to find now that no one was home at the Propersi house. From Doreen's yard, Franko could see Joey out in his driveway working on a car and decided to go talk to him since he had partied with the kid in the past. "Hey Franko, do you want to smoke some pot?" the teen asked, greeting his older friend. "Sure, why not. I've got some time to kill," responded the older man. The boy pulled a homemade pipe from his jeans pocket and said, "The place is crawling with cops, so let's smoke it in my car." The pair sat for the next few minutes, taking hits from the pipe while music blared from the car stereo. Joey's voice finally broke through the music, asking Franko, "I know where a keg party is tonight. Do you feel like coming?"

Kenny Comcowich pulled up in front of the driveway of the new house with his mother in the car. Walking up the driveway, he softly said to

Joey, "Ditch the weed, my mom is watching." He then asked, "Do you have a carburetor I can have for my car, Joey?" "Maybe I can rip one off from that station wagon parked in the street when the cops get out of the neighborhood tonight; it should fit your engine," Joey said to his friend, apparently unbothered by the prospect of committing a crime in a neighborhood awash with state troopers.

"Let's check the garage. Maybe there's a carburetor on the floor somewhere," Joey said to Kenny as they walked up the driveway to the new house. "So, did you see on TV what happened to Cookie's kids?" Comcowich said as the boys searched the garage for the desired auto part. "Yeah," Joey responded. Something snapped into Ken's mind as he stood there with Joey. Comcowich turned to Joey and said, "I think you did it." Joey just kept looking for the carburetor, not offering any response to his friend's charge.

Bob and Phyllis headed with the boys for dinner at Revello's on Main Street in Old Forge. The silence as the group sat in the booth gave way to tension. "You looked worried. What's the matter?" Joey asked his father. "This thing with the Ziemba children has me worried," Bob Aulisio responded. "You think I had something to do with it, don't you!?" Joey shouted at his father. "I swear to God, Dad, I couldn't do something like that," the boy added.

"We don't think you did it, Joe. It's just that we love you and we are concerned," Bob Aulisio said. Bob felt ashamed that the thought had crossed his mind. Bob decided to drop the whole thing and hoped they would catch someone before people around town started to attempt to place blame on his son. It was not a healthy situation around the trailer park with all the State Police and talk of murder in the neighborhood. The whole thing seemed to have Joey really stressed out, so Bob decided to bring him to the boys' uncle Joe's house for a change in scenery.

A fear gripped Mike Nalevanko that he had never known in his life. The thought that a killer lurked in Old Forge and, worse yet, could be just about anyone was more than enough to make him paranoid. The fears of a firefighter were well known to Mike, such as collapse of burning buildings or smoke inhalation. This situation was different from all others he had encountered; now there was a fear of the unknown. Mike felt ridiculous carrying a gun and looking over his shoulder as he walked to his girlfriend's house that night, but at least he would not be caught off guard by anyone.

For "Stosh" Zoltewicz, sleep did not come easy despite the fact that he had been awake for the last seventy-two hours. It was impossible to erase from his mind the vision of the little bodies of the Ziemba children covered

Searchers in front of Corey Slope, July 27, 1981. *Lackawanna County District Attorney.*

by pieces of discarded carpet. Stosh thought of his own son and wondered how anyone could do such a thing to a pair of helpless children. Stosh sadly concluded that Old Forge was "snakebitten."

Mike Jordan found the situation with the press out of control and interfering with the investigation. Press vehicles followed State Police cruisers throughout the county in the hopes of gaining information. To leave the shadow of the press for a meeting with his investigators, Jordan and Corporal Mernich boarded a police Blazer and then led the reporters on a chase across Lackawanna County. Leaving the press behind, Jordan and Mernich were able to meet with the other investigators in an isolated cemetery to discuss what leads to follow.

Dr. DiMaio's autopsy and the State Police evidence team had found several items that could narrow down the search for the killer. The children's clothing revealed blue and white rug fibers matching the rugs found on Corey Slope and at the pit. Metal and glass fragments of a blue-silver color were found on the bodies and the carpets. The investigators did not doubt that such fragments could be found at the murder scene.

Each investigator went and reviewed the investigation made during the day and outlined the evidence thus far uncovered. Pictures had been taken randomly of the entire neighborhood and now were being checked for any possible clues.

Examining one such photo, Trooper Nick Genova stopped and stated, "I was at that house today. It belongs to Bob Aulisio." "Anything turn up, Nick?" Mike Jordan asked. "I was walking on the property when a kid named Joey came from out of nowhere and asked what I was doing. I asked if the house had been searched, and the kid told me it had been on Sunday night by the searchers and that nothing had been found. I told this kid that I wanted to look around, so he opened up the garage door for me and gave me a tour of the place. The house isn't finished yet, and the kid said his family would be moving into it once the electricity was hooked up."

"Did you find anything in there?" Jordan asked. Nicky Genova replied, "The downstairs is pretty much filled with junk in both the garage and the adjacent room. The upstairs doesn't have any furniture in it, and there wasn't anything that didn't seem too out of order except for an awful odor of gasoline throughout the house. Bob Aulisio came on out and talked with me for a few minutes and said the smell must have come from gasoline from one of the cars his sons were working on in the garage. I told him that they should open a few windows and air the place out, and Bob said he would."

"Bob Aulisio and I go way back," Genova continued. "We grew up and went to high school together, and he used to make fun of my build, saying I looked like the Greek god Hector."

Trooper Gaetano recounted how he, accompanied by Trooper Padula, followed up the leads regarding the carpet found with the bodies up at the stripping pit. The State Police Wyoming Crime Lab determined that the white shag carpet, technically known as "Notorious Harmony White," was made by a Georgia manufacturer and only sold by one supplier in Lackawanna County, DiRienzo Carpet. The carpet company reported that this type of rug had most recently been installed for an individual residing on Summit Avenue in Clark's Summit just north of Scranton. It turned out that the individual who had bought the carpet had moved, selling the house to its present occupant.

The man who now owned the Clark's Summit home allowed the troopers to search the premises and to match the carpet found on the mountain with the rug in the dwelling's bedroom. Gaetano and Padula found the carpet to be similar in all respects to that which was found with the bodies.

It seemed certain that the killer had an intimate knowledge of the neighborhood. It was logical to assume that the suspect resided somewhere in or nearby the trailer park. The rugs found with the bodies and up on Corey Slope would be exhibited to each person questioned in the hope that somebody would recognize them.

THE RAID

The headline in the morning edition of the July 29, 1981 *Scranton Tribune* read, "Help Catch a Killer," pleading with those who had any information about the murders to come forward to the State Police, District Attorney Preate or even their clergymen. The Old Forge Bank was now offering in the newspapers a substantial reward for information leading to the arrest of the killer of the Ziemba children. Members of the community set up the "Ziemba Fund" to help the family pay funeral expenses for their children.

Trooper Gaetano and Padula were assigned to head to the trailer park in Old Forge and conduct interviews to identify the carpeting found up on the mountain. As they walked down Seaman Lane, Gaetano yelled to Padula to stop at a dark-brown trailer outside of which sat a white Plymouth Cricket. Trooper Gaetano was out of the police cruiser for about five seconds when a young kid with thick glasses confronted him, asking several questions in quick succession. "What are you doing here? What do you want? What are you looking for?" The kid's intensity startled Gaetano, who used the occasion to ask the youth, who identified himself as Joey Aulisio, some questions.

The trooper asked Joey when was the last time he had seen the Ziemba children. The teenager told him that he had last seen them playing on the empty trailer pad just down the street from his family trailer on Sunday around 4:00 p.m. When asked if any other troopers had interviewed the teenager, Aulisio said he "had been questioned by lots of policemen."

Joey's father came out of the trailer and joined in on the conversation. Bob Aulisio recounted the events of Sunday and noted that "Hector," Aulisio's childhood nickname for Trooper Nicky Genova, interviewed Joey and conducted a search of the house. "Everything seemed OK to Hector," Bob confided.

The workers at the DeNaples auto wrecking yard had earned their pay during Tuesday evening, having matched the tinplate of the carpet with a type of automobile. The dashboard cut-out was for a 1971 Plymouth Cricket, with some additional cut-outs for some types of accessories. The report came to Jordan at the command post, and an order was relayed to the troopers on scene at the trailer park that under no circumstances was the Cricket on the Aulisio property to be allowed to be moved and that the automobile was to be impounded if necessary.

One name kept coming before Troopers Gaetano and James as they walked the Connell's Patch neighborhood asking residents what they knew about the disappearance of the Ziemba children. The name was Joey Aulisio. Joe Lilli told the troopers that he remembered he had last seen the Ziemba children at about 4:00 p.m. on Sunday when he was leaving his trailer to go get a bite to eat at Snack and Putt on Main Street in Old Forge. Lilli remembered Cheryl and Christopher riding their bikes on the vacant trailer pad between his trailer and the Aulisio trailer before the children came to his door seeking to play with his daughter.

A teenage boy, Tim Dunnells, and his mother approached the troopers. Tim explained that he used to be a friend of Joey Aulisio's until the boys had a falling out. Joey then turned a group of boys against Tim and had been tormenting him for the past year. The teenager told of Aulisio torturing animals, including blowing up a baby 'possum with fireworks. Tim also claimed that Joey had broken into the family trailer and stole his stereo, leaving a note that said, "Thanks for the stuff, Tim."

Tim Dunnells's mother told of obscene phone calls that she would receive from Joey Aulisio, asking Mrs. Dunnells if she "wanted to fuck." Mrs. Dunnells also told the troopers that when she drove by the Aulisio property, Joey would pull down his pants and laugh as she was going by. She also said that she stopped going to the police about Joey Aulisio and stopped complaining to the boy's father because it only seemed to escalate Joey's torment of her son.

More neighbors told of Joey throwing rocks at Little League baseball players from Corey Slope down onto the ballfield below. The troopers interviewed that Little League coach whom Joey tried to hit with a hammer earlier in the year.

Doreen Propersi froze in horror as Troopers Gaetano and James Padula unraveled the blue carpet found with the bodies of Christopher and Cheryl. Doreen let out an involuntary gasp as she examined the carpet. "If this isn't the carpet I gave Joey back in May then it is its twin," exclaimed Doreen.

Propersi told Gaetano and Padula how back in early May she had been cleaning out her basement and Lenny along with Cookie Ziemba removed the old blue rug. And Joey came over from his yard and asked for the rug to use as a floor in his "bunk," which was the log cabin that he had built.

Any doubt in Doreen's mind regarding Joey's involvement in the murders was removed when the troopers showed her the bloodstained white shag carpet that had been cut out in the shape of a dashboard. Tears began to roll from Propersi's eyes as she began to shake uncontrollably. This was the rug that Joey had glued to his dashboard back in early July. The boy had been so proud of his customized dashboard that he came over to Doreen's and brought her over to his garage to show off his accomplishment.

Trooper Gaetano now knew that he could narrow his suspect list down to Joey or Bobby Aulisio. Gaetano immediately called command post, relaying Propersi's statement to Mike Jordan.

Ernie Preate wanted to speak directly to Doreen, as he knew her from growing up in the neighborhood and figured that she would trust him. The reporters present swarmed around Preate as he spoke to the now hysterical women on the other end of the phone. The command post froze in silence as the press listened to Preate's end of the conversation. "Did you ever see that carpet before?…What kind?…Which one?…When did you get rid of it?… Did you give it to him?…Is he the big kid?…Tell that to the police.…Calm down. I know you're broken up."

Preate and Larry Moran hurried to obtain search warrants. Michael Jordan quickly issued orders to the troopers from the command post. They were ordered to always know the locations of both Joey and Bobby Aulisio.

Trooper Walter Carlson observed Bobby Aulisio sitting in his car by the Aulisio trailer with Myron Jenkins. Carlson and Trooper James walked up to the boys and asked if they had heard anything more about the Ziemba children. Bobby did not tell the trooper any new information other than relating an inventory of the guns his family possessed—a 12-gauge shotgun belonging to Mr. Aulisio, along with a 20-gauge shotgun.

Bobby seemed friendly to the troopers and asked if there were any clues about who had murdered the children. The teenager then asked what would happen to whoever murdered the kids and if the children had been cut up or molested. Whenever Carlson directly asked Bobby Aulisio about the children, he would become evasive and attempt to change the topic of the conversation.

Carlson and James walked away from Bobby and met with a trooper who had been standing on the corner of Seaman Lane and Hard Street. The group walked up to the front of the Aulisio house when they were immediately confronted by Bobby Aulisio, who had walked over from his trailer and was now glaring at the state troopers. "What the fuck are you looking at?" Bobby growled. Then he began picking up empty discarded motor oil cans littering the Aulisio driveway.

"State troopers are following me and Joey everywhere we go," Bobby Aulisio complained to Robert Colburn. "Me and Joey just got back from Burger King, and the troopers followed us as we walked down Drakes Lane and all the way down Main Street." Bobby continued, "Everywhere I go I see state troopers!…That guy who had been talking to me before—Carlson— I've seen him and some other troopers out on Seaman Lane staring at the Cricket and looking inside it."

Bob Aulisio could not get the idea out of his head that Joey was somehow involved with the kids. Bob had continuously been asking Joey whether he had anything to do with the children. "Honest to God, Dad, I couldn't hurt those kids—they play with my brothers—I play with them," was Joey's reply each time Bob posed the question to him.

Bob thought back over the events of the last few days and tried to pin down what had been going on with the boys. Bob had been out late Saturday night at the St. Stanislaus Church picnic, even seeing Diane and her children there, and then went over to Francesco's in Moosic, getting back home around four o'clock in the morning.

On Sunday morning, Bob got up and went over to Chelland's Market before it closed to get some food for himself and the boys. Dominick, Patrick and Mike were visiting for the weekend, riding their bikes back and forth between Bob's mother's home on Sussex Street and the trailer. Bobby was at a softball game, while Joey had been hanging around the house and at one point went over to the softball game when his brother came back for him. Joey came in the trailer after he got back from the softball game to get a screwdriver and then went back out.

Bob next saw Joey sitting on the trailer porch at about 5:30 p.m. that afternoon. Bob was fuming that Bobby was still not back from the softball game and went to take the Cricket over to the ballfield and fetch him. Joey told him that he could not take the car because the oil pan was busted, but Bob took the car anyway, only to find Bobby already on his way home.

Even though Bob had told Joey to stay on the property, both he and Bobby searched late into the night for the children. On Tuesday, Bob went over to the new house twice to check for damage, since all sorts of people had been through the neighborhood since Sunday night, and found that his tax records had been scattered all over the floor.

For the State Police, careful planning would be necessary for taking the Aulisios in for questioning and searching their property. Pennsylvania law noted that any statements made by an individual in custody of the police for more than six hours, without an arrest occurring, were inadmissible at trial. Thus, within six hours, the Aulisios would have to be taken to the Dunmore barracks for questioning, read their Miranda rights and interrogated. If the Aulisios stayed tight-lipped for six hours, the job of finding a killer would become much more difficult.

Those witnesses questioned thus far by the State Police had indicated to the investigation teams that there were at least two shotguns and three rifles on the Aulisio property. Since a small arsenal was at the disposal of the prime suspects in a multiple murder, surprise would be the key element to the success of the operation. Strict silence regarding the operation would have to be maintained, without word of what was about to take place being leaked to the press. A meeting was held at the Dunmore Barracks at 5:00 p.m. with the State Police, local police chiefs and fire chiefs outlining the operation, now scheduled for 9:00 p.m.

Preate and Assistant District Attorney Larry Moran were before District Justice Riden at 3:00 p.m. requesting search warrants for the Aulisio property. Justice Riden, faced with an overwhelming amount of evidence indicating probable cause that a crime had been committed, issued search warrants.

J.R. Davis sat nervously with his mother, Sandra, in the Dunmore State Police Barracks, waiting to be questioned about Joey. Trooper Chester Kuklewicz, State Police youth officer, and Trooper John Atapovich questioned the fourteen-year-old. J.R. told the troopers that he had last seen the Ziemba children at about 3:50 p.m. on Sunday. J.R. had been sitting in the Aulisios' green jeep with Patrick and Mike Aulisio when the Ziemba kids came by and asked if they could sit in the jeep. Mike Aulisio told Cheryl and Christopher that they could not sit in the jeep, and they went off to Jessica Lilli's trailer. J.R. had then gone into his trailer with Patrick Aulisio and watched a western on TV until about 5:30 p.m. J.R. related that after a quick dinner he was back outside riding a minibike with Mike and Pat Aulisio at about 6:00 p.m., when Chester Ziemba came by to ask Bobby Aulisio for help finding the kids. From that time until 5:30

a.m. the next morning, J.R. had been helping to look for the children. Joey and J.R. were sitting in the Aulisio jeep at about 5:30 a.m. that morning because Joey was afraid to return home so late.

J.R. went home at about 6:00 a.m. to get something to eat, with Joey telling him to come over to his trailer in about twenty minutes to get him. When J.R. went to get Joey about twenty-five minutes later, there was no answer at the trailer or the new house, so he assumed his friend had fallen asleep.

"Did you ever see any off-white carpeting around, J.R.?" Trooper Kuklewicz asked, showing to the youth an off-white shag carpet cut in the shape of a dashboard. "Joe Aulisio put that type of carpet on the dashboard of his white Cricket on or about the 6th of July. He put it on with Elmer's Glue and made cuts to fit the speedometer, the buttons for the defroster, the warning lights and the eight tracks," J.R. responded.

J.R. Davis continued, "The white Cricket has a black interior—he took this off the dashboard about two days later. This carpet was left over from Mr. Aulisio's bedroom and was stored in the garage—when Joe ripped the carpet from the dashboard, he put it back in the garage." He added, "Did you ever see a dark-blue rug around?" Staring at the floor, the boy said, "Joey Aulisio had a dark-blue rug in his bunk which is to the rear of his trailer—he took it out about two months ago and put it in the new house, first putting it in the garage section and then into the house itself."

The ringing of Stosh's Fire pager broke the stillness of what had been a few hours of relative peace at the Zoltewicz home. All firefighters were to report to the Old Forge Hose Company immediately. Upon arrival at the firehouse, Stosh headed for the mini-pumper and again teamed up with Ed, Mike and Frank. Something having to do with the Ziemba children was happening down at the trailer park. "They must have a line on somebody down there," Mike said to Stosh as he turned the mini-pumper down Drakes Lane.

Old Forge Hose's engine blocked the intersection of Main Avenue and Drakes Lane, while the mini-pumper was assigned to the corner of Drakes Lane and Hard Street. The firefighters were assigned the job of crowd control on Drakes Lane. Television news crews were broadcasting a major break in the Ziemba murder case. The net effect of these broadcasts was to bring in droves of people to Drakes Lane. People were lined up five deep for the entire length of the road.

Darkness was descending on the neighborhood as firefighters parked an engine on the corner of Seamen Lane and Hard Street, setting up search

Crowd of onlookers surround the Aulisio property, July 29, 1981. *From the* Scranton Times-Tribune, *via the Lackawanna County Historical Society.*

lights aimed at the Aulisio property. State Police cruisers were lined up on either side of the fire engine, with troopers standing ready.

A voice from the crowd shouted, "They are going to give them so much time to come out and then they're going to start shooting." A helicopter seemed to hover directly above the corner property as the crowd grew silent. Suddenly the spotlights of the fire engine parked on Hard Street sent beams of blinding light at the trailer. "This is the State Police," was heard over a loudspeaker.

"Do you know you are surrounded?" Bob Reynolds of the local television news asked Bob Aulisio, who had just picked up the telephone on its first ring. Bob Aulisio's chest heaved as he looked out the trailer window into the blinding light of floodlights. "What should I do?" Bob Aulisio shouted to the reporter. "Just stay on the line," Reynolds replied, telling the television viewers, "I hope the State Police don't shoot like when they killed Robby Phillips," referring to a recent incident when state troopers shot a suspect during an arrest.

There was a pounding at the door, followed by the words "This is the State Police." Bob Aulisio looked helplessly to the door and then to Bobby and Joey, who, along with Myron Jenkins, were watching television in the next room. Tears began to fill Bob's eyes as he opened the door to see Nick Genova and a State Police lieutenant standing in the doorway. "Hector, what is this all about?" Bob Aulisio asked Genova.

Troopers Gaetano, Padula, Carlson and Mike Jordan stood in the trailer doorway, ordering Bob to put down the phone. Carlson grabbed the telephone and screamed into the phone, "Are you trying to get someone killed, Reynolds!?" Jordan said, "Mr. Aulisio, we have here warrants to search your property in connection with the murders of Cheryl Lynn Ziemba and Christopher Ziemba." "You don't need a search warrant. You can look anywhere you want; I have nothing to hide," Bob replied intensely. He began to cry in heavy sobs as Joey sat nervously on the living room couch holding a pillow between his hands. Joey finally looked up from staring at the floor and said to Trooper Gaetano, "Are you here to search the new house?"

Upon the reading of their Constitutional rights, the Aulisios were led out of the trailer to waiting State Police cruisers. Troopers Gaetano and Padula were to take Joey in one car, while Troopers Genova and Carlson were assigned to transport the other two. The Aulisios walked out of the

Aulisio family members taken into custody, July 29, 1981. *From the* Scranton Times-Tribune, *via the Lackawanna County Historical Society.*

Ernest D. Preate Jr. outside the Aulisio home, July 29, 1981. *From the* Scranton Times-Tribune, *via the Lackawanna County Historical Society.*

trailer and entered a world of confusion, blinded by the floodlights of a fire truck and surrounded by state troopers, with the flashes of cameras filling the night air.

An ambulance sped down Hard Street, leading many in the crowd to speculate that someone had attempted suicide. The ambulance was called in to aid firefighter Bobby Hughes, who had been struck by one of the floodlights atop the fire engine.

A convoy of State Police vehicles snaked down Drakes Lane, transporting the Aulisios to the Dunmore State Police Barracks. People in the crowd started to cheer at the State Police as the convoy made its way. "Hang the motherfuckers!" was yelled from the crowd, while others yelled, "Do to them what they did to the children!" Less creative members of the multitude contented themselves with yelling out "Kill them!" or simply "Bums!" One man standing close to the Main Avenue intersection held up a sign reading, "Bring back capitol punishment," apparently unbothered by the misspelling.

THE INTERROGATION

There was a knock on the door of Claire Aulisio's apartment. A neighbor said, "Do you know your house is on television?" Claire Aulisio turned on her TV to see the home that she left three years before surrounded by State Police. The broadcast said that Joey, Bobby and Bob had been brought down to the State Police Barracks in Dunmore in connection with the murders of the Ziemba children.

Troopers Gaetano and Padula arrived at the Dunmore Barracks with Joey just before 10:00 p.m. A crowd had already formed around the building hoping to catch a look at the suspects. During the trip up to Dunmore, a message came over the radio from the evidence team searching the Aulisio property. "You're on safe ground for arrests," crackled the message. Bobby Aulisio broke down in uncontrollable sobs. "Bobby knows something about what the evidence guys found," Carlson said to himself, thinking, "We've got about six hours to get something that can be used in court."

Once led inside the barracks, the Aulisios were separated, with the father and Bobby being held in one room, while Joey was held in another. Joey was read his rights and was asked by Gaetano whether he wanted an adult present for his questioning. "I want my dad here," the youth responded. Bob Aulisio was brought down from the office he was being questioned in. Just as Gaetano appeared with Bob Aulisio in the interview room, Claire Aulisio stood at the door, introducing herself.

Claire stared at Bob and silently mouthed, "I told you he needed help a long time ago." The stare from his ex-wife became more than Bob could tolerate. "Why are you making me out to be the prick? Why am I always the prick?" Bob yelled at Claire.

Joey sat quietly between his arguing parents. Gaetano again read Joey his Constitutional rights, handing the waiver of rights form to the teenager for his signature. Joey and his mother signed the rights form and handed it back to the troopers when bickering began anew. "Who are you to play God, you fat fucking cunt?" Bob Aulisio yelled, breaking down in tears. Nicky Genova led his former high school acquaintance out of Gaetano's office and attempted to calm Bob down.

Gaetano advised Joey of his rights one final time, saying, "I want to advise you that you have an absolute right to remain silent, and anything you say can and will be used against you in a court of law. Now do you understand what I just told the both of you?" Joey and his mother affirmed that they understood his rights. Trooper Padula asked Joey whether he ever had any pieces of blue carpeting. Joey said that he had some blue carpet but had thrown it away up on the mountain during the past winter. When asked about white shag carpet, Joey indicated that he had also thrown a white rug away during the winter. Gaetano asked Aulisio if he was sure that he threw the carpet away during the winter, to which Joey said there was snow on the ground when he disposed of the rugs. "Joey, we know that you couldn't possibly have thrown the carpet away during the winter because we know you didn't receive it until April or May." Aulisio quickly changed his story, saying only that he threw the carpeting away "just a long time ago."

Aulisio's mother encouraged, "Answer their questions—tell the police what you know." Claire tried to console Joey: "It will be all right—it will be all right." Joey began to cry. "Honest, Mom, I wouldn't do anything to those kids—they played with my little brothers. I played with them." "Joey, tell them what you know about the children," Claire repeated.

Joey's eyes filled with tears, and he said, "All right, I was framed....It was about six o'clock Sunday night—it was fucking disgusting, I went into the new house, and in the bedroom, there was blood all over the place," Joey told the state troopers. Gaetano feverishly attempted to write down the youth's statement as he continued. "I figured I'd better clean up before I got in trouble—my father found the shotgun in the closet."

Trooper Padula interjected, "Why did you clean up?" Joey responded, "I cleaned up because I figured I would get in trouble." Trooper Padula asked Aulisio, "What about the gun—which gun was it?" Quickly the boy answered, "It was the one that was missing—the shotgun that was missing finally turned up." "What about the bodies?" Padula continued. "There were no bodies—there were no bodies," Aulisio said in response. "What time was this, and why did you go up there?" Padula asked the sobbing teenager. "About six o'clock—I always go up there," Joey replied. Spontaneously, to no directed question, Joey said, "Oh God, it was fucking disgusting—I'll never forget it as long as I live—when I walked into that house it was like a horror movie—somebody was trying to frame me, but I caught on, I caught on!" As Aulisio made this last statement, he stared straight at Trooper Gaetano with a face the officer later described as "a strange otherworldly look."

Trooper Nicky Genova waved from the office doorway and motioned Gaetano out of the office. "An attorney has showed up downstairs saying he represents the Aulisio family, so you better cut the interrogation off now," Genova told Gaetano. "Nicky, we're within a few seconds of a full confession," Gaetano replied. "Walt Carlson is downstairs checking if this lawyer is legitimate—in the meantime, stop the questioning so we don't taint what we already have," Nicky Genova advised.

"I represent the Aulisio family, and I want all questioning of any family member you have here to cease this minute," attorney Mike Batista told Trooper Carlson. Batista was the attorney of Bob Aulisio's mother, who ran a dry cleaner in Old Forge. Mrs. Aulisio, alerted by the television news coverage, had hurriedly called Batista at home and had him rush to Dunmore to represent her son and grandsons.

"You can't represent the Aulisios in this, Mike—you're the Old Forge borough solicitor and that's a conflict of interest," Carlson replied to the lawyer. "I think I can represent him," Batista responded. "No, you can't—you're the borough solicitor. You represent the Old Forge Police Department—I'm not letting you see them," Carlson replied. "Well, you mark the time I arrived here—I'm going to get John Dunn of the public defender's office here," Batista responded. "So close to a complete confession," Carlson thought to himself.

Between his fits of crying, Bob Aulisio seemed to point a finger of guilt at Joey. Bob told Trooper Carlson, "I don't know, but for some reason I've had it in my head that Joe was somehow involved with this thing with the Ziemba kids….Joey had lost all fear of me recently; if he is involved in this thing, it must be the drugs he uses."

Public defender John Dunn arrived at the Dunmore barracks, immediately telling the desk officer to mark the time of his arrival. Dunn was no stranger to controversial cases, having represented William Wright in his murder trial for the Freach-Keen murders. "I want all questioning of the Aulisios to stop until they talk to me," Dunn told Carlson. Carlson walked to Gaetano's office and told the trooper to cease all questioning of Joey Aulisio. "Let's not lose what we have," Carlson told his fellow trooper. Dunn conferred with Joey Aulisio and announced, "My client will not answer any further questions."

A throng of about five hundred people milled about in the parking lot and on the lawn of the Dunmore barracks. The crowd occasionally dashed across the front lawn as State Police cruisers entered the barracks driveway returning from routine patrols to the disappointment of the throng that hoped for more news.

TELEVISION CREWS WERE SET up in the barracks parking lot, awaiting further announcements from the State Police. Dozens of members of the press lined the front steps and driveway of the barracks awaiting some word from beyond the glass-plated door. The crowd followed the events by reports aired on television monitors set up by various television stations on the front lawn of the barracks.

Many in the crowd shivered from the unreasonably cool night air as they watched *The Love Boat* from the television monitors between special reports on the Ziemba murders. Reporters questioned members of the crowd as they held a vigil outside the barracks. "I was just watching television and decided to come out and see what was going on," explained Jim Rice of Avoca to a reporter. A woman told the same reporter, "I'm just here because I feel bad for the family."

Inside the barracks, Ernie Preate conferred with Jordan and Carlson about which members of the Aulisio family would be placed under arrest. Joey Aulisio's statement was in and of itself enough for probable cause to make an arrest. "Joey Aulisio is definitely the shooter," Carlson said, adding, "The rugs and his statement make that clear." Nick Genova smiled with some satisfaction and said, "I told all of you the carpets would be the key." "Let's see what the evidence guys say before we announce an arrest," Preate said, staring out the window into the milling crowd.

The first discovery made by State Troopers Bill Rovinsky, Andy Merenich and Frank Zanin in their search of the Aulisio property was the lack of electrical power in the new house. The handheld flashlights brought by the troopers were insufficient for the task at hand so portable floodlights powered by generators were provided by the firefighters of the Old Forge Hose.

Rovinsky, Merenich and Zanin entered the new house and were immediately confronted by a Ford Pinto sitting silently in the garage bay. "Do you see that, Frank?" Rovinsky motioned to Zanin, pointing to the garage floor where a piece of white shag carpeting stood. A closer examination of the carpet revealed bloodstains. Shining their lights along the side of the automobile, the troopers could clearly see that something had been dragged along the floor to the door.

A doorway stood between the garage and a stairway leading upstairs. Crawling on his hands and knees, Rovinsky discovered a large bloodstain at the entranceway. Methodically, the trooper scraped up a portion of the stain with a pair of tweezers, placing the collected sample into an evidence bag. Rovinsky made his way on his hands and knees up the stairway, taking care to examine each stair with his magnifying glass. There was clear evidence on each stair that something had been dragged down the stairway, as a trail of blood mixed with blue metallic particles was evident. It seemed that someone had tried to mop or wipe down the stairs.

Something was visible on a stair, and Rovinsky, using his tweezers, was able to work the object loose. Holding the object up to the light, Rovinsky beheld a fragment of human skull. As Rovinsky worked his way farther up the stairs, he discovered at the top landing a piece of human flesh wedged in the floorboard.

Rovinsky followed a trail of mopped debris into what appeared to be a living room/kitchen area. A large, noticeable stain stood near the stairway on the living room floor. The trail of bloodstains and blue-colored glass fragments along the floor led from the hallway and into the master bedroom. Rovinsky was struck by the smell of putrefied blood. The stench of death permeated the room, as Bill Rovinsky turned to his fellow troopers and said, "This is the death scene."

The swath of mopped blood was followed to the closet of the master bedroom that ran the length of the wall. Two folding doors, marking each end of the closet, stood partially opened. Rovinsky noticed immediately upon looking into the closet that a toggle light switch had been broken off from the wall. An Eagle-type toggle switch had been discovered by the State Police Crime Lab in the brain matter that had been found up on the culm bank.

Skull fragments on stairs at the "new house." *Lackawanna County District Attorney.*

Box of Christmas ornaments, from the death scene. *Lackawanna County District Attorney.*

"My God, we found a light switch up on Corey Slope—this has got to be where it happened," Trooper Rovinsky said, adding, "Look down there, a box of broken Christmas tree ornaments. I guess that's where the fragments came from." The box of ornaments stood on the right side of the closet floor, and it appeared that the entire back wall had been washed down by someone.

Closet floor showing blood behind baseboard. *Lackawanna County District Attorney.*

Despite his years as a criminal investigator, Rovinsky could not hide his shock when he examined the second closet door, discovering that it was covered with wiped-down blood and clumps of hair. The troopers removed the door from its hinges for forwarding to the crime lab and carefully removed a few strands of the hair for further examination.

Rovinsky noticed a spent shotgun pellet in the far corner of the closet. The smell of putrefied blood was overwhelming, as Rovinsky removed the closet wall floorboard, revealing a pool of still congealing blood. The floorboard was covered with strands of hair.

The Aulisio trailer was an unremarkable structure painted brown and white. Trooper Frank Zanin entered the trailer home, taking immediate note of a beige blanket with horse and Indian designs sitting on a couch.

Near the trailer's front door stood the door to a small bedroom in which yet another horse and Indian blanket sat on a bed. The bedroom was typical of most trailer homes, being small with a combination dresser and closet built into the wall. "They told me this is Joey Aulisio's room," Rovinsky said as he examined the area around the bed, pulling a cigar box from underneath.

Rovinsky examined the contents of the cigar box that he had emptied onto the floor. Several spent and live 12-gauge shotgun shells spilled onto the floor, one of which appeared to be covered with blood.

More live and spent shells were found by Rovinsky crammed into the top dresser drawer. Stickers advertising motor parts and spark plugs covered the walls throughout the bedroom, prompting Rovinsky to say aloud, "This kid sure loves stickers." The blanket found on Joey's bed stood out to the

Trunk of Plymouth Cricket with bloodstains. *Lackawanna County District Attorney.*

troopers since it represented an exact match to the blood-soaked blanket found up on Deater's Lane.

Rovinsky turned his attention to the Plymouth Cricket parked alongside the trailer home. The car was small and was painted a dull off-white, which gave it the appearance of a refrigerator on wheels. Blue and white metallic particles were visible throughout the trunk. A can of DuPont carburetor spray sat in the trunk that revealed a drop of blood on one side. The carpet in the trunk of the vehicle consisted of an old blue rug like the one found with the children's bodies.

Utilizing his magnifying glass, Rovinsky discovered two long strands of hair just to the left side of the spare tire. "Want to bet this belongs to Cheryl Ziemba," Rovinsky commented. When the spare tire was lifted, more fragments of blue-white glass were discovered underneath in the wheel well. Rovinsky matched the dashboard-shaped piece of white carpet against the car's dashboard to discover that it was a perfect fit.

A tow truck arrived to drag the Cricket to the barracks in Dunmore for further inspection. "Some night they had up in Dunmore," the driver of the tow truck said to the troopers as he exited his vehicle. "It got really wild out there—it really looked like the crowd would string that kid up on their own—you guys really missed the action."

"I think we were where all the action was," Rovinsky replied.

JOEY STOOD SILENTLY AS a State Police photographer took front and side profile pictures. Occasionally, a tear would cascade down his face as the arguing voices of adults echoed. "Your client is being charged with two counts of murder and two counts of kidnapping," Ernie Preate yelled at public defender John Dunn, who in turn argued that there was no basis for holding any member of the Aulisio family.

It was the opinion of Carlson that Bobby Aulisio had not been involved in the murders but was an accessory after the fact. The trooper theorized that at some point on Monday, July 27, 1981, Joey admitted his involvement to his brother, who in turn helped him dispose of evidence.

It was necessary to arraign Joey, and District Justice Eiden of South Scranton was contacted to prepare his courtroom for his arrival. Frank Talerico, the district justice sitting in Old Forge, could not be located. Therefore, Eiden would have to substitute.

A precession of vehicles followed a line of State Police cruisers to the South Scranton courtroom of Justice Eiden. Troopers Gaetano and Carlson sat with the handcuffed Joey Aulisio in the back of a police cruiser. Joey sat silently through the ride, clutching his glasses in his handcuffed hands and wearing a red varsity-type jacket given to him by his uncle just prior to leaving the State Police barracks. The youth seemed passive and unemotional as the cruiser pulled into the Judicial District Court's parking lot surrounded by angry crowds. Carlson found Joey's nonchalant attitude disturbing, thinking to himself, "There's something not right about this guy."

The mood of the crowd of onlookers turned when the convoy arrived at Eiden's courtroom. People pounded the police car with their fists as it slowly made its way into the parking lot. Carlson and Gaetano, surrounded by two dozen troopers and Scranton police, made their way with Aulisio to the building's entrance, followed by hostile shouts of "Fry him!"

"Kiss my ass!" Joey yelled back at the horde, breaking the silence he had held since leaving the barracks. Before either Gaetano or Carlson could stop him, Joey threw his glasses onto the ground, smashing them underneath his shoes, prompting Carlson to yell out, "The little son of a bitch is smart—he knows he can be identified by his big glasses."

Joey looked out of place standing at the defendant's table in the courtroom. Preate read the charges aloud to the court: two counts of murder in the first degree, two counts of kidnapping and two counts of hindering prosecution. Joey nodded and whispered a soft "yes" when asked by Eiden if he understood the charges. His public defender, Dunn, requested Aulisio be held in the Lackawanna County Youth House rather than the jail. Preate replied that the seriousness of the charges required Joey be held in the most secure facility in the area: the Lackawanna County Jail. Eiden ruled that Joey would be held at the county jail.

Mike Jordan gazed out the window at the crowd growing by the minute. Shouts of "Hang him!" emanated from the crowd and echoed in the small courtroom. Jordan was scanning the parking lot to determine the best way out when he noticed a car blocking the exit. "Whose car is that?" Jordan shouted. Dunn answered, "It's mine." "Well, move it unless you want your client to be ripped to pieces by that mob."

The public defender pushed his way into the crowd toward his car to the shouted insults of "Asshole!" Troopers Carlson and Gaetano led Joey out the door toward the waiting police cruiser as the mob surged forward.

The first shot rang out, sending ice down the spine of Trooper Carlson as he pushed Joey headfirst into the back of the cruiser, trying as best as he could to shield the suspect. Gaetano slammed the car's door shut, shouting, "Drive!" The trooper behind the wheel pushed his foot to the gas pedal and sped away with a convoy of other police cruisers as a second shot rang out.

The crowd scattered in all directions, hiding behind cars and the court building. Scranton policemen and state troopers pulled out their sidearms and scanned the area for a gunman. Television reporter Mary Keating picked herself off the ground, noting the smell of gunpowder in the air, and slowly realized that the "gunshots" were actually firecrackers. The police, with pistols drawn, continued to scan for the phantom gunman before finally noting the source of the explosions and holstering their weapons.

It was nearly four o'clock in the morning when Joey was led into the jail. Procedure at the Lackawanna County Jail dictated that all new arrivals would be subjected to a physical examination. Aulisio was forced to strip for examination by the on-duty prison paramedic, who noted that there were no cuts or bruises on the new inmate's body. Joey was then issued a pillow and a blanket before being led to the isolation cell.

A TOWN SNAKEBITTEN

Alan Hoover followed the current events by habit. When there was news of significant events, Hoover would often save the article from the newspaper. When President Reagan was inaugurated, Alan deemed it to be an event worthy of saving the entire newspaper.

The music of John Lennon had always been important to Hoover, so he saved articles regarding Lennon's assassination. Similarly, a dogfight between American F-14 fighter planes from the aircraft carrier USS *Nimitz* and Libyan MIGs warranted the saving of articles since Alan's brother served as a sailor on the carrier. Throughout the week, Hoover followed the news about the Ziemba kids on the radio and took care to save the daily newspaper articles.

Alan had stayed up late on Wednesday evening, July 29, 1981, to watch the television coverage of the arrest of Joey Aulisio but, uncharacteristically, ignored the newspaper the next morning. Returning home after a day's work in the summer heat on the afternoon of July 30, 1981, he settled down to read the paper. A picture of Joey Aulisio adorned the newspaper's front page, and after a quick scan, Alan turned to page three to follow the lead story. Hoover felt his stomach turn as the article stated that a small white economy car had been confiscated when Joey Aulisio had been arrested. Alan Hoover had a hunch about the whole thing and reached for the phone to call Tom Scoda. "Bring the paper with you tomorrow when I pick you up for work, and then we'll talk about it," Scoda told his friend.

The next morning, the honking of a horn from Tom Scoda's pickup truck stirred Alan out the front door for the trip to Fitchburg Coated

Products, where Alan worked as a packer and Tom was employed as an electrician. Alan thrust a newspaper clipping into Scoda's face and said, "Before you do anything, read this—just thinking about it kept me up all night." "Was that part of the mountain in Old Forge—I thought we were still in Duryea?" Tom replied after carefully reading the article. "Maybe when we crossed the Stephenson Street bridge on the way up the mountain we were in Old Forge," Hoover responded. "My foreman is an Old Forge fireman. Let's talk to him when we get to work, maybe he'll set us straight on this," Tom Scoda replied.

John Alimenti had just punched into the time clock when Tom Scoda approached and pulled him aside to talk. "John, are you still active in the fire company down in Old Forge?" Alimenti uttered an affirmative grunt and asked, "What do you need to know?"

"Well, Al Hoover and I were up in the mountains at the stripping pits late Sunday afternoon, and we saw a kid driving a little white car up the road only to come back down again a few minutes later—he seemed shocked to see us up there, as though he had seen a ghost." Alimenti's eyes bugged open wide. "Tommy, I think this is important—can you tell me more about this car?" "I'll do better than that. I can draw it for you. I really paid close attention to the car's front grill—can't say I ever saw anything like it before," Tom responded. Utilizing a piece of scrap paper, Scoda drew a very near likeness of the white Plymouth Cricket that had been confiscated by the State Police. After studying the drawing for a moment, Alimenti said, "Tommy, would you and Alan be willing to talk to the State Police?" "If you think it is important," Scoda replied. "I think it's very important, Tom," Alimenti said as he took another look at the drawing.

Troopers Padula and Carlson arrived at Fitchburg after having received a call about someone having important information regarding the Ziemba murders at the plant. Hoover and Scoda told their story to the troopers, convinced that they had been dumping brush in a totally different area from which the bodies had been found. To the surprise of both, the troopers were not only interested in what they had to say but also requested that the pair accompany them to look over some evidence that had been recovered.

Padula and Carlson first escorted Alan Hoover through the barracks garage and then returned for Scoda. The garage contained about twenty to thirty cars, parked along a walkway down the center of the structure.

Carlson motioned to one car and said, "That's the car we confiscated the other night." Scoda looked at the auto for a second and walked farther down the parking spaces, stopping to point at a small white car and saying, in almost the exact words used by Alan Hoover but a few minutes before, "That may be the car you took in, but this is the car Al Hoover and I saw up on the mountain." Carlson glanced an affirmative stare in the direction of Padula, as now both men had correctly picked out Joey Aulisio's Cricket without any coaching.

Both Hoover and Scoda were shown photos of various teenage-looking boys wearing thick glasses. Alan Hoover was able to correctly pick out Aulisio from the photos; however, Tom Scoda was less sure of himself.

The morning *Scranton Times* sat at the edge of his driveway, and Stosh Zoltewicz picked up the paper and glanced to see the headline "Old Forge, a Town Snake Bitten." Stosh stood in the driveway wondering whether if the paper was correct. Surely, the Ziemba children were "snakebitten," thought Stosh, but could an entire town be?

A white casket sat silently in the parlor of the Samuel Palermo Funeral home in Old Forge holding the remains of Cheryl and Christopher. There had been no viewings held, as the Ziemba family wished the final hours before interment to be private. A pall of gloom consumed the bright August 1, 1981 Saturday morning as the pallbearers slowly carried the casket to a waiting hearse destined for a St. Stanislaus Catholic Cathedral in South Scranton.

Ziemba family friends Ron Cistola, Andy Dudeck, Johnny Matthews, Stephen DuBeras, Greg Taroli and Mike Schuback served as pallbearers. Schuback reflected on how he had fixed an oil pan for Bob Aulisio on Tuesday.

Just prior to the procession leaving the funeral home, one of the pallbearers walked up to the army of reporters lined up on Main Street and requested that no questions be asked the Ziemba family. The twenty-car funeral procession then snaked its way through Old Forge to St. Stanislaus, followed by a multitude of reporters.

The hope of the Ziemba family to remain out of the spotlight was shattered upon the procession's arrival at the church, as television cameras filmed each move made by the mourners. The bells of St. Stanislaus rang sporadically as Diane and Cookie Ziemba stepped out of their car, with Cookie attempting to comfort Diane. A teenage girl, one of the curious onlookers to the scene, wore a T-shirt reading "I survived Main Street Old Forge." The television cameras stopped following the couple as they entered the church, followed by the pallbearers and the casket of little Christopher and Cheryl.

Cookie and Diane seated themselves in the front pew as the choir filled the cathedral with strains of a processional hymn. Diane clutched Cookie's

Casket carrying the bodies of the Ziemba children at the funeral. *From the* Scranton Times-Tribune, *via the Lackawanna County Historical Society.*

hand as she cried, her head resting on his shoulder. The sight of the grief-stricken couple proved to be too much for supposedly hardened members of the press corps, who found themselves weeping. Ernie Preate sat in a pew near Diane and Cookie Ziemba, as the spectacle wrenched the heart of the battle-hardened former marine.

Bishop Rysz commenced the mass of the angels and then was joined by the Very Reverend Edward Abramski, Cheryl and Christopher's great-uncle. Bishop Rysz read several passages from the Bible pertaining to children followed by his own thoughts regarding the tragedy that had befallen the Ziemba family. Rysz implored those gathered for the funeral, "I bid you petition the Lord of Creation to free us of the violence and depravity which has become so much a part of our lives....We bemoan this violence, and we are frightened by it." Turning toward Cookie and Diane, seated in the front pew, Rysz went on to say, "We have lived through a tragedy which completely altered the life of Chester and Diane for it has taken their children, their heritage which was of the Lord, for fruit of the womb is God's special gift....It has altered the life of the youth in custody of the authorities and his family—it has altered the life of our community as a whole."

Gazing toward the left side of the church, Diane and Cookie stared at the casket surrounded by candles. Abramski spoke briefly, referring to Joey Aulisio as "that vicious person." With service concluded, those congregated for the funeral slowly funneled out of St. Stanislaus for the short trip to the Sacred Heart Cemetery off Davis Street in the Minooka section of Scranton. The bells of the cathedral began to ring once again, filling the air with a melancholy sound that seemed to drive the press with their ever present television cameras a respectful distance from the mourners.

Silence enveloped the cemetery as the Ziemba family, mourners, clergy and the press walked to the grave site. Mourners, the press and onlookers

Cookie and Diane Ziemba at the funeral. *From the* Scranton Times-Tribune, *via the Lackawanna County Historical Society.*

were silent, refraining from even the slightest whisper when the children's great-uncle Reverend Abramski commenced the short graveside service.

"We are also here to manifest our love and concern for Chester and Diane—words cannot adequately covey the sense of loss and grief which we feel, but our presence here manifests our support of those whose loss cannot be measured in any human terms," Abramski observed, addressing the mourners. The lily-white casket containing Cheryl and Christopher was placed on the bier, and the mourners seemed to move instinctively toward the source of their grief.

Cookie and Diane, shrouded in black, sat nearest to the casket, she with her head on his shoulder, he clutching her right hand with his. Abramski threw a handful of dirt on to the coffin, and the choir began to sing "God Be With You" as the grief of the day reached a crescendo, with tears becoming the common link of all those in attendance. Cookie and Diane got up from their seats, approaching the casket for the last time, with the young mother bending down to the coffin's lid and gasping "Goodbye my darlings" as she softly set a flower down.

The emotional sight of the grief-stricken mother saying her final goodbye to the children ripped at members of the news media, as each began to break down into tears. One at a time, cousins, aunts, uncles, friends and strangers stood in line to each lay a single flower on the bier.

The crowd slowly followed Cookie and Diane Ziemba to the waiting cars as the young couple, leaning on each other for support, started home to try to pick up their shattered lives. A few people stayed behind to watch the cemetery workmen lower the casket into the ground. A man observing the burial commented to a reporter, "At least they never felt anything."

ATTORNEY JACK BRIER WATCHED with disapproval the television news showing the taking of the Aulisios by the State Police for questioning. Normally an operation of this type would have been kept from the press until the very last moment of execution. Obviously, an advance warning had been given to the media. The warning of the State Police raid on the Aulisio home was a dangerous thing.

Jack Brier did not excel as an attorney by accident, but rather his prowess was the result in a lifetime of achievement. This life carried through Jack's days as a high school basketball star to his undergraduate studies at the University of Scranton.

CRIMINAL PROCEDURE

Jack Brier early on concluded that the overall best strategy he could employ would be to have the courts treat Joey as a juvenile offender. Being charged as an adult would open Joey up to a life sentence with no possibility of parole. The District Attorney's Office could seek the death penalty against Joey.

Initially, a preliminary hearing was scheduled in Joey's case for August 7, 1981. In Pennsylvania, a preliminary hearing is a procedural hearing before a local district justice to decide whether there is sufficient evidence to charge an individual with a crime. The standard to be met by the District Attorney's Office in a preliminary hearing is only that there is evidence that a crime occurred and that there is sufficient evidence to charge a particular individual with a crime.

Brier immediately petitioned the Court of Common Pleas to adjourn the preliminary hearing and transfer the case against Joey to the Juvenile Court. Brier, in his petition, argued that Joey's "need for care, guidance and control as a juvenile outweighs the need of society to apply legal restraint and discipline to him as an adult." Brier's petition requested the court grant a juvenile hearing to determine Joey's "need and amenability to the program of rehabilitation."

Common Pleas Court Judge S. John Cottone, a former U.S. attorney and a new judge to the Common Pleas Court, was initially assigned the case and questioned Brier regarding why he had not served the district attorney with

Aulisio's petition as required. "I didn't inform the District Attorney's Office because I didn't want Ernie Preate to notify the press," replied Brier.

Judge Cottone's law clerk contacted Preate about Brier's filing of the petition. Preate was livid upon hearing Brier's allegation that he would contact the press. Within an hour, Preate had delivered to Judge Cottone a reply to Brier's petition that denied that Joey's "needs outweigh those of the Commonwealth and society and that he should not be considered a child under the law."

Judge Cottone considered the petition by Brier and signed an order adjourning the preliminary hearing. Judge Cottone also scheduled a hearing for whether the charges against Aulisio would be heard in Juvenile Court for September 8, 1981.

A petition of another sort was circulating, but not within the court system. Ronald Gallagher of Taylor circulated a petition urging the "maximum penalty be sought for the person or persons responsible for the brutal murder of the Ziemba children." Gallagher's petition concluded, "We believe this is necessary for the protection of all children."

Be it a petition against Joey or the icy stares of neighbors, Bob Aulisio was feeling the pressure of public opinion since the raid. Bob withdrew his candidacy for a seat on the Old Forge School Board. He and Bobby had moved into Bob's brother's home in Taylor.

Although Judge Cottone was certainly a capable jurist, Lackawanna County President Judge Edwin Kosik wanted a more experienced judge to be assigned to the Aulisio murder case. Accordingly, Judge Kosik invited Judge James J. Walsh to his chambers to discuss Walsh being assigned the case.

Judge Walsh was a man of accomplishment. A football legend at West Scranton High School and football scholarship recipient at Washington and Lee University, Walsh interrupted his studies after two years to enlist in the U.S. Army during the Korean War. Following military service, Walsh then returned to his studies and football at Washington and Lee. Following graduation, Walsh received his law degree from Georgetown University Law School.

Returning home from Washington, D.C., James J. Walsh, a Democrat, plunged into local politics. First Walsh was elected to the City of Scranton School Board and eventually became school board president. In 1965, Walsh was elected, at age thirty-five, the youngest mayor in the history of Scranton.

In 1969, Walsh ran for reelection and for the first time crossed paths with Ernie Preate. Preate served as one of the operatives of Republican Eugene

Peters's campaign against Walsh in the November 1969 election. It was a bitter, hard-fought election. Walsh lost reelection to Eugene Peters, not in small part due to the efforts of Preate.

In 1971, a vacancy arose on the Court of Common Pleas in Lackawanna County, and Governor Milton Shapp appointed Walsh to fill it. In 1973, during the same year Scranton Mayor Eugene Peters won reelection, Walsh was elected by voters to a full ten-year term.

Ernie Preate's tenuous relationship with Judge Walsh continued during his serving as an assistant district attorney throughout the first half of the 1970s. Preate's election, in his own right as district attorney in November of 1977, brought the two men in more contact than either of them would have wished.

Walsh ordered a psychologist to examine Joey Aulisio to assist the court regarding whether to treat the teenager as a juvenile offender or as an adult. Under then existing Pennsylvania law, if it could be proven that a minor offender could be rehabilitated by the time he or she reached the age of twenty-one, the individual would be deemed a juvenile. A murder conviction as a juvenile would, at worst, cause Joey to be incarcerated only to the age of twenty-one and any conviction record would be sealed from the public.

State Police investigators were kept busy during the month of August 1981 attempting to fill in the blanks regarding the personality of Joey Aulisio to prepare the District Attorney's Office for the scheduled hearing about Aulisio's juvenile status. What was discovered during interviews with Joey's friends and neighbors was disturbing. Allegations were made of Aulisio drowning a cat in gasoline, burying animals alive and torturing a kitten to death by covering the animal with auto bondo.

Both Kenny Comcowich and Robert Colburn told of Aulisio capturing a baby 'possum in a trap, tying an M-80 firecracker around the animal's neck and then releasing the creature to have it then be blown up. Both Comcowich and Colburn told the state troopers that the most disturbing aspect of the incident was Joey laughing hysterically after the incident. The blowing up of the baby 'possum was one reason, Comcowich explained, why he had concluded that Joey had murdered the Ziemba children.

Two forensic psychologists examined and conducted tests on Joey Aulisio: Dr. Gerald Cooke and Dr. Robert Sadoff, the head of clinical psychiatry at the University of Pennsylvania retained by Jack Brier on behalf of Joey. Both Cooke and Sadoff were to testify at the juvenile status hearing regarding their findings.

Dr. Gerald Cooke found based on his interview and tests that there was neither "mental retardation nor major mental disorders" with Joey. Cooke also found that Aulisio did suffer from a "conduct disorder," ranged in severity from "mild to moderate." Cooke also concluded that Joey Aulisio was "undersocialized." Cooke's tests revealed that Joey had an IQ score of 81, in a range of "dull-normal."

Dr. Robert Sadoff concurred with Cooke regarding Aulisio's IQ and undersocialization. Sadoff found a more dominant and less meek Joey Aulisio than did Cooke. Joey felt, according to Sadoff, that males were superior and that females were only good for sex and to "make ready for men." Dr. Sadoff also found that although Aulisio was dull, he had no major psychological disorders. Dr. Sadoff noted Joey's continued truancy from school as a possible cause of his low IQ.

On Tuesday, September 8, 1981, Joey left the Lackawanna County Jail, under heavy guard, and entered the courtroom of Judge Walsh. Wearing a light-blue pullover sweater, Joey Aulisio sat with Jack Brier at the defense table. Both Dr. Cooke and Dr. Sadoff were called to the witness stand by Brier.

Cooke urged that although Aulisio would need extensive therapy, the teenager could be rehabilitated by the age of twenty-one. Cooke testified that he could not classify Joey as either "aggressive or nonaggressive."

Ernie Preate attacked the credibility of Dr. Cooke. Confronting Dr. Cooke with more than a half-dozen instances of Joey's alleged torture of animals, Preate demanded of the psychologist to answer whether these incidents with animals would change his mind about whether Aulisio was "aggressive." For each instance cited by Preate to Cooke, the psychologist admitted that it would make him "believe" Joey was aggressive.

Dr. Sadoff took the witness stand following Cooke. Sadoff, with his testimony largely echoing Dr. Cooke's, despite Preate's questioning, reiterated his findings to the court. Sadoff expressed the opinion that Aulisio could be rehabilitated.

Dr. John Hume, a psychiatrist retained by the District Attorney's Office, also had examined Joey Aulisio and testified in rebuttal. Hume's findings contrasted sharply with the opinions of Sadoff and Cooke. Hume testified that Joey had every characteristic of an antisocial person and but for his youth would have so classified Aulisio.

Dr. Hume noted Joey's poor relationship with both his mother and father. Hume expanded on this point, testifying that Aulisio had anger for his father, directing his anger at children and animals that were small and helpless. Hume testified that Aulisio's torturing of cats was a "malignant prognostic sign."

Joey glared at Kenny Comcowich and Robert Colburn as each testified regarding repeated instances of Aulisio's torture of animals. The testimony of sixteen-year-old Tim Dunnells was damning. Dunnells testified that Aulisio had placed kittens in a box and connected a hose from the box to a car exhaust, killing all the kittens. Dunnells also testified that Aulisio had threated to "blow off the head" of Dunnells's eight-year-old brother.

Bob Aulisio testified in rebuttal; however, his testimony did more harm than good for Joey. Bob admitted Joey killed a cat with exhaust fumes, but it was only one cat and not several cats.

Judge Walsh ruled, in his opinion, that "although the evidence may indicate a need of a program of supervision, care and rehabilitation, this Court is not convinced of the amenability of this defendant to such a program. I find in balancing the young offender's need for care, guidance, and control as a juvenile against the interests of society, and the need for adult discipline and legal restraint in cases of crimes of such a heinous nature, the needs of the public and society outweigh this young individual's needs."

With Judge Walsh's opinion, Joey Aulisio would now be treated as an adult by the courts. The preliminary hearing would now take place on Thursday, September 17, 1981. Due to security concerns, the hearing was moved to the Olyphant Borough Building.

A preliminary hearing is conducted by a district justice who is essentially a locally elected judge for a judicial district, usually encompassing one municipality. Typically, the district justice hears motor vehicle violation cases and minor criminal infractions. However, the district justice is also assigned to hear the more serious criminal matters for preliminary hearings, up to and including capital murder cases.

With Judge Walsh's decision, the determination regarding whether Aulisio would be bound over for a grand jury to hear the charges against him was in the hands of district justice, Frank Talerico of Old Forge. The hearing would prove to be the most serious of Talerico's tenure as a district justice.

TOM SCODA AND ALAN Hoover each took individual turns standing behind a two-way mirror at the Dunmore, Pennsylvania State Police Barracks to see if any of the suspects lined up against a chalkboard was the boy they saw driving on the mountain. Jack Brier was present and arguing loudly with

Lineup photo of Joey ("F"). *Jack Brier.*

Mike Jordan, refusing to allow Joey to wear glasses at the lineup. Jordan threatened to place Brier under arrest for interfering in a police investigation.

Kenneth Vercammen, a University of Scranton cross-country runner from New Jersey, sat in the lineup. Vercammen was in the lineup at the request of his cross-country coach, as there was need for thin young men with thick glasses to take part in the lineup. An unease came over Kenneth as he watched Brier and Jordan bicker. Kenneth wondered if he was sitting next to a killer.

The lineup scene that greeted Tom Scoda struck him as odd. Sitting before him in a police classroom were seven young men in combination chairs/desks like those used by grammar school kids, all wearing glasses, with the letters "A" through "G" drawn in chalk on a blackboard behind the boys, with a single letter pointed to each suspect.

It did not take very long for Tom Scoda to pick out the kid he saw on the mountain. Sitting under the letter "F," wearing a plaid shirt, was the boy Tom had seen driving up on the mountain. Alan Hoover picked out Joey Aulisio two out of two times. Mike Jordan nodded to Walter Carlson, certain that a major piece of the case against Aulisio had now been sealed.

THE ESCAPE ATTEMPT AND
THE PRELIMINARY HEARING

There was something particularly repugnant about Joey Aulisio in the mind of Trooper Walter Carlson. Carlson felt that if there was ever a suspect who demanded no sympathy, it was Aulisio.

Perhaps the sight of the shattered bodies of the little boy and girl at the bottom of the stripping pit turned Carlson's heart cold as far as Joey was concerned. Maybe it was the kid's demeanor that bugged Carlson, for as far as he could see, Aulisio was totally devoid of any remorse.

It was Carlson's job, along with Trooper Gaetano, to guard Aulisio during the preliminary hearing and to protect the suspect. Community sentiment against the Aulisio family was running at a fever pitch in Old Forge, with threats having been made against Joey's life and the dry cleaning shop his grandmother operated on Sussex Street.

A horde of reporters and photographers greeted Justice Talerico as he exited his car and headed into the Borough Building of Olyphant. Soon after Talerico's arrival, a convoy of State Police cruisers made its way through Olyphant escorting Aulisio to the hearing.

The reporters gave the troopers a wide berth leading Joey, dressed in slacks and a brown sleeveless sweater that hid a bulletproof vest, into the building. Carlson felt the shackled Joey Aulisio bump forcefully into him. Was it an escape attempt? A second such forceful bump provoked Carlson's response of slamming Joey onto the hood of a State Police cruiser and growling a warning: "Don't even dream of it."

Stosh sat in the back of the hearing room with Mike, Ed and Frank as the troopers led Joey to the defense table. It was for the men their first look at the

Joey being led into the arraignment. *From the* Scranton Times-Tribune, *via the Lackawanna County Historical Society.*

killer of the Ziemba children. Joey Aulisio was equally interested in getting a good look at the horde of people. Slowly, Aulisio turned his head and looked directly back at the firefighters.

Joey's attention turned to Ernie Preate. Preate focused his eyesight at Aulisio, projecting a look of disgust and contempt. Preate stopped and spoke in hushed tones to Cookie Ziemba, once again giving assurances that the murderer of his children would not escape justice. After a brief opening statement, Preate called Cookie Ziemba as his first witness.

Cookie Ziemba first testified about the events of Sunday, July 26, 1981. Ziemba spoke of coming home from working the night shift and later having his daughter ask if she could go out to play with her brother. This proved to the last time Cookie ever saw his children alive.

Alan Hoover testified spotting Joey on the mountain at approximately 5:00 p.m. on July 26, 1981. When requested by Preate to point out the individual he saw up at the stripping pits, Hoover stood up, pointed his finger at Aulisio and stated, "I saw that person right there." Hoover stated that he "looked Aulisio right in the eye" when the youth drove by him.

J.R. Davis, Myron Jenkins and Ken Comcowich testified. J.R. Davis testified that he lost track of Joey after about 4:00 p.m. on the afternoon of July 26, 1981, and did not see Aulisio again until about 6:00 p.m. Jenkins also placed Joey Aulisio in the upstairs area of the new house for a significant period of the day on Monday, July 27, 1981.

Comcowich placed Joey on Sunday, July 26, in the new house after 6:00 p.m. apparently in the process of cleaning up something. Comcowich also told the court how he spotted a pool of blood.

Throughout the two-day preliminary hearing, Joey sat impassively. Occasionally, he would peer through his thick glasses at the bloodstained carpets presented as evidence to the court. On other occasions, Aulisio would stare directly at the witness who was testifying as though he was searching for some sign of weakness.

Frank Genell and Mike Nalevanko felt this cold stare of Aulisio as they testified regarding finding the bodies of the Ziemba children at the bottom of the stripping pit. Frank Genell still felt personally affected by his discovery. "I still can't it get out of my mind," he told the court.

When testimony concluded, Justice Talerico asked Jack Brier if he wished to put his client on the witness stand. Brier simply stated, "I demure to the evidence." Jack Brier in his closing statement requested dismissal of all charges against Joey Aulisio, arguing that no testimony showed that Joey had planned any murder, which was necessary for a charge of murder. Brier further argued that there had been no evidence of kidnapping.

Preate launched into his rebuttal to the court. Cheryl Ziemba had been shot in the head with a shotgun, and Christopher received a gunshot wound to the chest—"The killer's choice of those parts of the body gives rise to the inference that this was an intentional act." Regarding the kidnapping charge, Preate argued that the children had been taken into the unfinished house on the Aulisio property "without their parents' consent," which was enough to establish kidnapping because of their tender ages. "A four-year-old doesn't just go into a closet," Preate's words thundered as he stared directly at Joey Aulisio. Pointing directly at Aulisio, he shouted, "He tried to cover up the murder of those two children."

A numbing silence fell across the courtroom following Preate's rebuttal. Justice Talerico quietly shuffled papers on the bench for a moment, writing notes, and then paused, staring thoughtfully into the overcrowded courtroom. Talerico stated that in consideration of the facts and evidence before him, he had found "a prima facie case" (meaning the establishment of enough evidence) against Aulisio, who would be bound over for trial.

Claire Aulisio, now Claire Bohenek, having remarried, approached Joey with Bob Aulisio and shared a brief hug. Joey smiled and spoke a few inaudible words before being led away.

THE END OF THE preliminary hearing did not bring about an end to the courtroom appearances of Stosh, Frank, Ed, Rich or Mike. A few days after the hearing, the firefighters were served subpoenas to testify at a bail hearing for Joey Aulisio.

Jack Brier simultaneously filed petitions to set aside Talerico's decision and for a hearing to decide the issue of bail. Brier sought to have Joey released into the custody of his grandmother and his father. During the day, he proposed that Aulisio would work each day at his grandmother's dry cleaning establishment and that Bob Aulisio would tutor the teenager each day after he had returned from teaching.

Preate labeled the plan put forth by Brier to be "unworkable and dangerous especially since threats had been made against the Aulisio family." Preate stated to the media that Aulisio's "life could not be guaranteed" if the teen was released on bail.

On Monday, October 5, 1981, Judge Walsh began hearing testimony regarding the issue of whether Joey should be permitted bail. Testimony had been given by the Aulisio family regarding their plan to have Joey supervised while awaiting trial. Testimony was put before the court by Dr. Edward Brennan, a clinical psychologist, who testified that during this period, he would work with Joey in intensive therapy sessions.

Stosh, Mike and Ed testified about the difficulties that would be encountered by firefighters should there be a firebomb attack on Mrs. Aulisio's dry cleaning shop. All three testified that not many volunteers were available during weekday work hours for fire calls, a time in which it had been proposed that Joey would be working at the dry cleaners.

Ed Orzalek, as assistant fire chief, testified that the chemicals in a cleaning shop would present an especially dangerous situation for firefighters and that it could not at all be guaranteed such a fire could be contained to one building. This, coupled with the fact that at any given moment patrons could be in the dry cleaners at any time during the day, could lead to grave consequences, Orzalek testified.

Brier asked Judge Walsh for a conference following Ed's testimony and produced a recent copy of the *Scranton Times* publishing Preate's comments regarding Aulisio. After warning both Preate and Brier to discontinue the practice of trying the case in the newspaper, Judge Walsh instructed counsel to begin their summations. Brier immediately placed the reason Joey's safety could be endangered directly on the hands of Preate, arguing that he was "suggesting in the media ways Joseph Aulisio could be harmed." Brier suggested Aulisio, if granted bail, spend his time at a location known only to the court and defense counsel. Preate argued that Aulisio's release would present a grave danger. Preate urged, "We've got to be concerned for Aulisio and others if somebody comes into the dry cleaners with a shotgun or a firebomb."

Brier argued that Preate was trying his case in the media and had even gone as far as to suggest ways that Joey Aulisio could be hurt. Ernest Preate in reply quoted the testimony of Dr. Sadoff, the defense's expert forensic psychiatrist: "It would take five years of intensive treatment in a locked

121

unit before Joseph could return to society." Further quoting Sadoff, Preate continued: "Make no mistake, Joseph is a disturbed youngster."

Judge Walsh issued his ruling, finding that "bail would not be in the accused or society's best interest." Walsh found that it was entirely proper to deny bail when the death penalty could be imposed. Judge Walsh's decision was not the only setback that Jack Brier's case would sustain during the month of October. One week following the bail ruling, Brier once again stood before the court, this time a two-judge panel of Judge James M. Munley and Judge Walsh, to attempt to overturn the findings of District Judge Talerico. Brier argued that the preliminary hearing did not present evidence to substantiate a prima facie case regarding the murder and kidnapping charges against Joey.

Assistant District Attorney Joe Wright, making his first court appearance in the case, argued that sufficient evidence had been presented at the preliminary hearing. Wright noted, "Pennsylvania law indicates that kidnapping is committed when anyone takes control over a youth under age fourteen without parental permission." Both Judges Walsh and Munley agreed, upholding the ruling of Talerico.

Brier had traveled to Philadelphia to appeal the denial of bail before the Superior Court of Pennsylvania. Assistant District Attorney Joe Wright again argued that a complete denial of bail was indeed warranted. Superior Court Judge James Cavanaugh agreed with Wright's argument, upholding Judge Walsh's decision to deny bail.

FACING THE DEATH PENALTY

Preate now faced the moral question of whether to seek the death penalty against Aulisio. Joey's young age and his apparent troubled background had to be taken into consideration. Yet the pictures of the bodies of the Ziemba children brought home the reality of the savagery of the crime and diminished what sympathy Preate had for Aulisio.

The imposition of the death penalty on juvenile offenders was not rare in the history of the United States. Up until 1964, there had been a total of 281 executions of juvenile offenders. In June 1944, South Carolina executed fourteen-year-old George Stinney, who had been convicted of the rape and murder of two young girls. In 1948, sixteen-year-old Donald Frohner was put to death at the Ohio State Prison for a carjacking-murder he committed in Youngstown. Bernard Scriber was a seventeen-year-old who died in Ohio's electric chair in 1956 for a rape and murder outside Toledo.

In New York, three juveniles—William Diaz, Benitez DeJesus and Edward Haight—were executed on the same day in Sing Sing's electric chair on July 7, 1943. Diaz and DeJesus died for a mugging-murder of a soldier on leave in Harlem. Haight had been convicted of the rape and murder of two children in September 1942.

Pennsylvania's death penalty statue did not specifically preclude a juvenile offender from the death sentence based on age alone. While Pennsylvania had no juveniles under the penalty of death awaiting execution, several other states did, so it was not totally without precedent to seek the death penalty against Joey Aulisio.

The new year of 1982 broke cold and overcast with the announcement that the death penalty would be sought against Joey Aulisio. The announcement did not come as any great surprise to Jack Brier, as he believed that it fit in perfectly with the politics that now engulfed his client's case. Joey Aulisio was perhaps the most hated person in Pennsylvania. The media had portrayed Joey as evil personified, and it would be difficult to find a single person without a hardened opinion about the case.

Brier filed two motions before Judge Walsh to change the trial's location. Judge Walsh's review of videotaped news broadcasts and of newspaper articles clearly showed that it would be impossible to panel an unbiased jury in Lackawanna County. In consideration of the evidence presented before him, Walsh granted Brier's motion in February 1982 to change the location of the county from where jurors would be selected. Walsh ordered that the trial would commence the first week of May 1982.

Jack Brier was not pleased upon learning that a jury from Bucks County would hear the case against Joey Aulisio. Bucks County represented perhaps one of the most conservative juror pools in Pennsylvania. It was now for Jack Brier to go down to Doylestown, the county seat of Bucks County, and select a jury that would at least give his client a fair hearing.

THE HALLWAYS OF THE Bucks County Courthouse erupted into anger as words were exchanged when the Aulisio family and the district attorney's staff passed in the hallways. Ernie Preate heard "cocksucker" and "prick" hurled in his direction. It was not an ideal time to discuss a plea bargain with Jack Brier; however, Preate wanted to put an offer of guilty pleas in exchange for a reduced sentence on the table prior to a jury being selected.

"Plead him guilty to one count of first-degree murder and one count of third-degree murder and we won't seek the death penalty," Preate said to Brier as he leaned against a wall outside the courtroom. "Look, let's say the shooting of Chris was an accident—I'll give him that; Cheryl's murder was intentional. He hunted her down to eliminate a witness—maybe he panicked, but whatever happened, he meant to kill her," Preate added. "At least he'll have a chance for clemency in the future with this deal—he'll someday see the light of day. I'm telling you if the jury finds him guilty on all counts, they'll sentence him to death," Preate concluded.

"No dice," Brier shot back at Preate, adding, "You don't have the proof behind your case—it's all circumstantial and you cannot directly link Joey to these murders, and even if you get a jury to convict him, no jury will sentence a fifteen-year-old to death."

"I'm telling you, Jack, take this deal and save your client's life," Preate said, now standing inches from the face of Jack Brier. "Given the evidence I'm going to present to the jury, Joey has a one-way ticket to the electric chair," Preate said with his voice getting louder. "After this day, Jack, there won't be any more offers of a deal," Preate warned. Preate added, "While you're thinking about it, why don't you tell your client's family to stop with the threats and the name calling. It's not going to affect me in the least."

"No deal," were the only further words uttered by Jack Brier. Ernie Preate turned his back on Brier and slowly walked into the courtroom to begin the process of jury selection. A jury was selected encompassing a cross-section of the population of Bucks County. An unemployed construction worker, several housewives, a few retirees and several small business owners, among others, made up the jury.

"Mr. Preate, may I speak to you?" said a voice from behind Ernie Preate as he was leaving the courthouse. Turning like the former marine he was in an almost about-face, Ernie Preate discovered that the voice from behind him was Diane Ziemba.

Preate was shocked to see Diane Ziemba in Doylestown, as the strain of the deaths of Cheryl and Christopher had been so great, she had been unable to speak to anyone from Preate's staff. "What can I do for you Mrs. Ziemba?" Preate said in a soft voice, mindful of Diane Ziemba's fragile emotional state.

"There is something I never told you, Mr. Preate, and I never told anybody from the State Police either, and I really need to tell this," Diane Ziemba replied. "What is it, Diane? You can tell me," Preate said. "The day he killed my children…I saw Joey Aulisio from our apartment window walking Cheryl and Chris into the back of his house," replied Diane.

Shocked, Ernie Preate could only utter the first thought in his mind: "Why didn't you tell someone before?" A tearful Diane Ziemba replied, "It just hurt so much, Mr. Preate—you know I've never been able to go back to the apartment since this happened—I cry nightly and sometimes I talk about this with Cookie.…Anyway, a little while back, I told Cookie about this, and he told me I would have to come forward and tell you about it—I owe that much to our children.…It just hurts so much to talk about it, I haven't been able to tell you or the police before."

"Do you think you could testify—you know that will mean Jack Brier will be able to cross-examine you?" Preate said to the grieving mother.

"I'll have to. I owe it to my children the truth be known," Diane Ziemba responded. "Are you positive about what you saw, Diane?" Preate asked. "Yes, absolutely. I saw Joey Aulisio walk my children into that house, and that is the last time I saw them."

SCRANTON

Joey Aulisio sat alone in his cell at the Lackawanna County Jail on Sunday evening, May 9, 1982, rereading a letter he had recently received that interested him more than his impending trial. Joey could now boast that he had a girlfriend. Laura Hueston, a seventeen-year-old from Dunmore, had been corresponding with Joey from early on in his stay at the Lackawanna County Jail. Joey and Hueston maintained a relationship by correspondence, as he was not allowed visitors other than immediate family and legal counsel.

Aside from television, Joey's main form of entertainment had been piecing together jigsaw puzzles brought to the jail by his father. Joey had spent so much time with these puzzles that he memorized them. After piecing together some of his favorite puzzles, Joey glued the pieces together and taped the puzzles to the wall of his cell as though he was hanging works of art.

Ernie Preate and Jack Brier glared bitterly at each other as they sat in the chambers of Judge Walsh on May 10, 1982, the first day of the trial. Judge Walsh entered his chambers and prepared to take what is procedurally called "offers" regarding what the day's initial testimony would be following opening statements by counsel.

Jack Brier also was less than happy about the way Preate proposed how he would present the evidence found on Corey Slope to the jury. Brier objected to Judge Walsh regarding the presentation to the jury of the brain matter and skull fragments, arguing that this would inflame the jury. Walsh ruled that although the brain matter was barred from presentation to the jury, the skull fragments could be presented as evidence.

Joey was led into the courtroom and seated at the defense counsel table. Seated alongside Brier was co-counsel Diane Beemer. Joey sat slumped in his chair, sporting a crisp new blue suit, uninterested in the goings-on in the courtroom.

Joey's interest in what was happening in the courtroom rebounded when Trooper Walter Carlson walked through the courtroom with a 12-gauge single-shot shotgun with an evidence tag attached to it. Joey quickly turned and stared at Bobby. Bobby's face turned ashen white, and he ran from the courtroom.

Carlson smiled to himself knowing that his ploy, discussed beforehand with Mike Jordan and Preate, had worked. The shotgun, although identical to the murder weapon, was not the shotgun owned by Bob Aulisio. Rather, Carlson had tracked down an identical shotgun purchased in

Joey being led into the courthouse, May 11, 1982. *From the* Scranton Times, *via the Lackawanna County Historical Society.*

March 1967 after Bob Aulisio had purchased his shotgun at Sears. Carlson had, through a records search, tracked down the identical gun's owner, who had consented to the shotgun's use for the murder investigation and trial.

Carlson speculated that given his behavior prior to the arrest of his brother, coupled with the information given by an informant from the county jail, Bobby Aulisio had disposed of the murder weapon at some point during the search for the Ziemba children at the request of Joey. Bobby's reaction in the courtroom seemed to confirm Carlson's theory.

Jordan realized that Joey was sitting at the defense table with his middle finger pointed at him under the table. Mike Jordan turned to Aulisio and said, "Hey Joey" before making a gesture of pulling a switch, and then he made the sound of an electrical current. Joey Aulisio's eyes bugged out, and his face turned distinctly pale in color.

Jack Brier elected to defer his opening statement until after the case against Joey Aulisio had been presented. Thus the jury would first hear of the events of July 26, 1981, through the opening statement of Preate. His opening statement lasted seventy-nine minutes, so long, in fact, that Judge Walsh permitted a recess to allow the jurors a short break.

PREATE COMMENCED HIS OPENING, stating, "The charges are grave, and this matter is serious." Then he moved to the events of July 26, 1981. Preate spoke of Old Forge to the jurors and went on to describe Corey Slope. "Culm is coal waste—it was thrown and piled there fifty to sixty years ago—it's useless and nobody wants it," Preate told the jurors.

Ernie Preate next set about weaving Joey into the scene as the boy who lived next door to the Ziemba family. "Joseph's father was building a house next door to the Ziembas—it was Joseph Aulisio's private domain."

Preate told the jurors that at "5:00 p.m. on July 26, 1981, Cheryl and Christopher Ziemba were first noticed to be missing. Soon volunteer firemen were called out and began to search for the children at Hard and Oliva Streets because that's where Joseph Aulisio told the police to start looking. As dawn began to break over this little borough there was a discovery of bloody carpet, a plastic bag, sandals, and brain parts on Corey Slope by a man and his wife."

With full fury in his voice, Preate continued: "Joseph Aulisio drives a car even though he is only fifteen years old—he gave four different accounts as to how the oil pan on his car was broken on the day the kids disappeared."

Preate set forth the physical evidence of the case. "Let's go back a step—there was blue carpet found with the bodies of the victims on July 28, 1981. Their little bodies were found thrown like garbage at the bottom of a strip mining pit—found by five volunteer firemen. These firemen had systematically checked the strip mining pits on the mountain side and when checking the second pit Frank yelled out for Stanley—'Stosh, Stosh,' [as] he had found the bodies.…[Regarding the] blue carpet found with the victims you will hear Doreen Propersi testify that she gave it to Joseph Aulisio months before the children disappeared. A white shag carpet, cut in the shape of a dashboard, was also found with the victims— you'll hear kids from the neighborhood testify that this carpet belonged to Joseph Aulisio."

Preate then guided the jurors through what had happened on the night the State Police arrested Joey. "You will hear the language that Joseph Aulisio used to describe the scene at his father's house, and it is not very nice—it's his own words, not mine."

"Now where was Joseph Aulisio after those kids disappeared?" Preate asked in a rhetorical question. "Two people were dropping off debris at the strip mining pits at 5:00 p.m. that Sunday afternoon—you'll hear their testimony—and lo and behold what do they see—a white Cricket automobile and who do they see driving but Joey Aulisio."

Preate turned toward Joey and continued, "We intent to strip him, piece by piece of his innocence, fiber by fiber, glass ornament particle by glass ornament particle, pellet by pellet, photo by photo, eyewitness by eyewitness, drop of blood by drop of blood."

Immediately, Preate motioned the court that Joey Aulisio be required to wear his glasses throughout the trial, stating, "That's how he can be identified—he always wears them—he's blind as a bat without them—we watched them lead him into the Courtroom today it was obvious that he could not see a thing."

Gazing a malevolent look toward Jack Brier, the district attorney continued, "I don't understand why you're trying to hide this kid's glasses." Judge Walsh ruled that only for identification only would Joey Aulisio be ordered to wear his glasses in court.

The first witness presented to testify was George Hughes, fire chief of the Lawrenceville Hose. Pointing to a photograph of a narrow dirt trail, Hughes testified that on the evening of July 26, 1981, he drove up to the top of Corey Slope looking for the children. Preate pointed to a plastic bag visible on Corey Slope and asked whether Hughes observed it during his Sunday night search. Hughes replied that he had seen neither the plastic bag nor the blue piece of carpet during the night search.

Mark Stillwagon testified that he served as a part-time Old Forge police officer and was at home on July 26, 1981, when he had heard commotion and went to Corey Slope to find out what was going on. Stillwagon testified as to the arm's length search of Corey Slope.

Hughes and Stillwagon made clear in their testimony that they did not see the blood-covered plastic bag or the blue carpet when each man had searched Corey Slope. Both witnesses stated that they had last been up on Corey Slope until around 4:30 a.m. on the morning of July 27, 1981.

Frank LaSota testified regarding searching Corey Slope on July 27, 1981, with his wife and of their discovery of a blue carpet covered in blood. LaSota testified about officers uncovering a red beach shoe and a child's pair of sandals that were stained with blood. LaSota remarked, "Ironically, they were dry," explaining that it had been raining. Diane LaSota in her testimony reiterated her husband's testimony.

Opposite: Joey led into the courthouse, May 10, 1982. *From the* Scranton Times-Tribune, *via the* Lackawanna County Historical Society.

Right: Joey arrives for trial, May 10, 1982. *From the* Times-Leader.

Sergeant Biaranccardi testified that on the evening of July 26, 1981, he put out an "all-points bulletin" and immediately requested the help of the firefighters from the Old Forge Hose to assist the search. Biaranccardi elaborated how he arrived at the trailer park and found a group of teenagers standing on the corner by Hard Street. Biaranccardi stated that he asked the teenagers if they had seen the Ziemba children, and Joey Aulisio indicated that he had last seen the missing children on the corner of Hard and Olivia Streets near Corey Slope. Biaranccardi testified regarding the thick glasses worn by Joey Aulisio that night. Judge Walsh ordered Joey to stand and don his glasses. Biaranccardi's testimony concluded with his discovery of a blood-covered blanket in the weeds off Deater's Lane.

The second day of trial, May 11, 1982, in Judge Walsh's chambers, juror number eleven stood trembling, requesting to be excused from the case. "If I get upset my heart goes fast—this thing kept me up all night," the juror pleaded.

Preate knew that a reluctant juror was potentially a very bad juror and said, "I don't want to create any problems for any individual—I think if the man is saying something, what can I do?" Judge Walsh excused the juror.

Ernie Preate had decided to rely on Ed Orzalek and Frank Genell to testify regarding the discovery of the Ziemba children. Orzalek testified

131

Sketch: Joey Aulisio at the courthouse with Jack Brier. *From the* Scranton Times-Tribune, *via the Lackawanna County Historical Society.*

that the State Police discouraged searching up on the mountain, telling Ed's group, "All right, we can't stop you if that's what you want to do."

Ed testified that upon reaching the top of the mountain, he along with Mike Nalevanko and Rich Besancon searched the pit on the south side of the dirt mountain road, while Stosh and Frank Genell checked the hole on the north side. "Frank then let out a scream and I turned to Mike and said I hope he didn't find them." He continued, "Frankie was holding his stomach and Stosh was telling him not to look….We stood over the side of the pit, and I could see the little white legs of the kids sticking out from underneath a blue carpet," Ed told jurors, who were now sitting on the edge of their seats.

The jurors again sat mesmerized as Frank Genell testified how the dirt road snaked its way from the end of Connell Street up the mountain; when the group reached the top, they doubled their way back down the road on foot, checking each strip mining pit. The group then searched the top two pits, finding nothing, with himself and Stosh moving on to the next pit.

"Who is Stosh?" Preate asked. "Stanley Zoltewicz," Frank Genell replied, continuing his testimony by stating that the group of firefighters drove farther down the mountain road and checked the next set of pits. Preate now had Genell identify an aerial photo of the strip mining pit.

Frank Genell bit his lip, reminded of the scene of horror when he was asked to testify about finding the bodies of Cheryl and Christopher Ziemba. Ernie Preate now had Genell identify a ground-level photo depicting the site where he had discovered the bodies. "This is the area where the children were either dumped, or thrown, or whatever," Frank Genell testified as he surveyed the picture, adding, "I could see that the girl's leg had some sort of red covering." "What did you do?" Preate asked the shaking young firefighter. "I walked away—I felt dizzy, upset and sick," Genell replied.

Trooper Rovinsky was a methodical individual who would review his pending testimony time and time again prior to testifying at trial. Rovinsky always suffered from a massive case of stage fright before testifying. On this day of trial, Rovinsky would prove to be unshakable.

Preate had Rovinsky identify a group of photos taken around the trailer park neighborhood on Monday, July 27, 1981. The photo clearly showed that on Monday, the Ford Pinto hood that had covered a pool of blood on Sunday evening, July 26, 1981, had been moved and was now leaning against the outside wall of the new house.

Preate had Rovinsky walk the jurors through exhibits found on Corey Slope. The trooper held up and identified for the jurors a newspaper-type plastic bag, now black from fingerprint dust; blood-covered children's shower clogs; a bloodstained piece of white carpet; a large piece of blue carpet; three pieces of a wooden chair; a child's sandal; a plastic piece of light switch; and pieces of human skull. Several jurors momentarily looked away from the evidence to cast angry glances at Joey Aulisio.

The carpet, Rovinsky testified, was discovered off a dirt road that ran up to the ridge of Corey Slope. About thirteen feet from the blue carpet was a piece of white shag rug. Rovinsky testified that he turned over the piece of white shag rug and noticed what appeared to be blood and a large amount of brain matter. The faces of the jurors seemed to be a study in horrified fascination upon this revelation.

THE TRIAL, DAY THREE

DIANE ZIEMBA TESTIFIES

Brier and Preate sat in Judge Walsh's chambers awaiting the start of the third day of trial on Wednesday, May 12, 1982. Jack Brier rose to his feet and spoke up: "Your Honor, I want on the record it was brought out by my co-counsel when the District Attorney was giving me two exhibits, he made faces at the defendant—the jury could see him—I request the Court direct District Attorney Preate to refrain from theatrical facial expressions."

Turning toward Brier's co-counsel, Diane Beemer, Judge Walsh asked, "Define threatening facial expressions counselor?" Diane Beemer said, "I would describe it as a deliberate attempt at intimidation."

"That's an awful lot of conclusions—nobody has asked me to say anything," Preate interjected. "You'll lie about it anyway," replied Jack Brier. Preate rose and shouted, "Your Honor, see how totally unprofessional this is!" Preate continued, "I turned around—no question about it—I looked at you [pointing his finger in Jack Brier's face], and I looked at the defendant—now if anybody wants to draw from that, I am threatening or intimidating—fine—that's your conclusion—you are not going to stop me from staring at whoever I like."

Preate's rage continued. "This is a free country and it's not Jack Brier's world that he can control—I'm getting a bit fed up Your Honor with all these insinuations of improper conduct in front of you putting it on the record."

"I think we can cut this off right here," Judge Walsh said, putting the matter to rest: "All Mrs. Beemer can describe is a stare—I don't see how there is any problem done."

Preate, satisfied with Judge Walsh's admonishment to defense counsel, proceeded to move on to his offer to the court of the proposed testimony for the day. "We're going to finish up with Trooper Rovinsky today and we are also going to be calling Mrs. Ziemba who will disclose when the last time she saw her children, with whom and where they were going." "When you say whom—who is she going to testify to?" Jack Brier asked. "Joseph Aulisio the defendant," replied Preate.

"Your Honor, I was never notified until last week of this witness and since I was not properly notified, I move that her testimony be excluded," Jack Brier demanded. Judge Walsh inquired, "Is there any reason for the late notice?"

"There sure is," Preate confidently replied, adding, "Nobody talked to her—this lady has gone through an ordeal—the only thing she ever said to me was that she wanted her picture back of her children—this information was disclosed during the course of jury selection and it was disclosed to Mr. Brier after she told me that."

"Based upon the explanation of the District Attorney I overrule the objection," Judge Walsh opined. Preate continued, "We also intend to call Doreen Propersi to the witness stand." "Will there be testimony of Joey's prior activities?" Jack Brier asked. "Like blowing up animals?" Preate said in a mocking tone.

Trooper Rovinsky's meticulous testimony regarding the evidence found on Corey Slope on July 27, 1981, and the items found in the search of the Aulisio property was presented to the jury. Bloody pieces of carpet, blood swatches and hair found in the new house and the blood-spattered folding door to the master bedroom closet were all presented to the jury.

The jurors again were sitting on the end of their seats in the jury box as they heard Rovinsky testify regarding the foul odor of "putrefied blood" while searching the master bedroom closet of the new house, characterizing the odor as "the smell of death." Rovinsky pointed out pinpricks of bloodstains on the folding portions of the door, explaining to the jury that the findings on the door further solidified his opinion that the master bedroom closet was one of the two "death scenes" in the new house.

Diane Ziemba walked to the center of the courtroom aisle and took a seat in the witness stand. The thin young woman of the past summer had been superseded by an individual with short-cropped hair dressed in a somber blue business suit.

Preate decided to start with simple questions to ease the obviously shaken mother into her testimony. When questioned regarding her residence, Diane replied, "We moved from the Drakes Lane house on the day I went into the hospital—I couldn't even go back for my clothes—I could not even step foot on the property."

"Do you have any children?" asked the district attorney. "Right now, no—I had a beautiful girl and one little boy," the grief-stricken mother answered.

Preate probed the afternoon of July 26, 1981, with his questions. "Could you look out the windows of your house?" "Yes," Diane answered, adding, "From both windows you can see the whole back of the trailer court, the culm bank, and in the winter, you can see as far as Mrs. Propersi's house, but not in the summer."

Regarding Sunday, July 26, 1981, Diane testified, "I told my daughter she better clean her room if she wanted to go outside, because she had certain chores she had to get done before she could go out. She cleaned the room and she got done and then she came over to me and she said, 'Mommy, the room is clean now, can I go out with Chris to play?' I said yes, she can go out, but make sure that you take care of him and watch him. And that was her job all the time—she watched over him. And I told her to make sure that she

Sketch of Diane Ziemba testifying. *From the* Scranton Times-Tribune, *via the Lackawanna County Historical Society.*

didn't go out of the area of the trailer court and stay where I could see her from a window, because that was what I always told her when she went out."

"Do you recall the last time you saw your children?" Ernie Preate asked Diane. "Yes, I do. The last time that I saw them, Christopher was entering the unfinished house on the Aulisio property. All I saw was the back of his head before he went into the house. Cheryl was a few feet behind him, and right in back of her was Joseph Aulisio and he had his hand on the back like this [Diane demonstrated how she was Joey's hand on Cheryl's back]. And before they went through the house, I saw Joseph turn around and look, and I thought it was—I don't know—I didn't see any reason why he should look because nobody was calling his name: there was no noise or anything. I thought it was a little bit odd, but I don't know, it was drizzling at the time, and I thought he was taking them in out of the rain. Maybe he was looking for somebody else. And that was the last time I ever saw them."

"What time was that?" Preate asked as a follow-up question. "Approximately four o'clock give or take a couple minutes either way," Diane answered with tears rolling down her face.

Those in the courtroom sat in a stunned silence, and about half of those in attendance were in tears after hearing her testimony. Seated near Diane was the Lackawanna County District Attorney's Office victim-witness coordinator, Nancy Baldwin, who was also in tears. Preate took a deep breath and continued his questioning of Mrs. Ziemba.

After having Diane recount for the jury her frantic search efforts, Ernie Preate questioned the young mother regarding her dealings after and before the children's disappearance with Joey Aulisio. "Did you see Joseph Aulisio after this time?" "I didn't see him until later on. I guess it was around seven o'clock and he was in front of his white car, and I asked him if he had seen the children, and he said no."

Ernie Preate walked toward Diane Ziemba and instructed, "The person that you saw taking the children into the unfinished house, I want you to identify him in this courtroom; stand up and point him out." Diane stood up slowly, focusing on the defense table, and extended her arm along with her index finger. With a slight quiver in her voice, she said, "It is Joseph Gerard Aulisio, sitting right over there in the gray suit, gray jacket, only he doesn't heave his glasses on."

Jack Brier now faced a herculean task in cross-examining Diane. It was abundantly clear, as evidenced by several crying jurors, that all who were in attendance in the courtroom felt great sympathy for the mother. An overly harsh cross-examination of Diane could practically guarantee a guilty verdict.

Jack Brier asked Diane, "Now, you indicated that you saw Joseph behind your children, and I think you indicated that his hand was on Cheryl's back as though guiding her toward the door. Is there a specific reason why you recall it was around four o'clock?" "At around four o'clock, I remember it, because I—a little after four o'clock, the telephone rang, and it was my grandmother, and I was talking to her," Diane answered.

Brier continued hammering home the theme that Joey Aulisio had permission by Diane Ziemba to bring the children into the home, asking Diane, "When you saw Joseph, as you indicated, taking them into the home, you didn't have any particular concern or anxiety at that point in time, obviously; did you?" Diane answered with a simple "No." Brier then asked, "So, at that point, you didn't object to Joseph taking them in the home on the apparent circumstance, as you indicated that he was taking them out—getting them out of the rain?" Diane replied with a "Yes."

Ernie Preate decided to take the step of recalling Diane to the witness stand for redirect examination to hit home the fact that she, as would any human being, was confused and frightened, thereby was prone to mistakes during questioning. Preate asked, "You have not been at any of the proceedings in any courtroom?" Tears rolling down her face again, Diane replied, "No, I couldn't."

"Have you tried to be here during this week?" Preate asked. "Yes," replied Diane. Immediately thereafter, Preate followed up with the question, "Have you been able to discuss this, any part of this incident, with anybody?"

Diane answered, "No, it's just so heartbreaking to have your only daughter, two children, and to know somebody killed them and to know that you're never going to see them grow up and you know that somebody killed them and took all those precious years away from me, and, for my own sanity, I just cannot think about this. I love my children very much and all their memories will always stay with me, but from July 26th on, I just could not cope with those memories. As a matter of fact, I couldn't even tell my husband."

Silence again fell on Judge Walsh's courtroom as Diane Ziemba walked from the witness stand and down the main aisle, which split the capacity crowd of spectators, to take a seat next to her husband. The tear-filled eyes of jurors, spectators and members of the press followed Diane on her short journey to Cookie, with no voices daring to breech the stillness. Joey Aulisio sat next to Brier looking as though he did not have a care in the world.

Preate now sought to bring the jurors' minds to the scene of the crime so they could visualize where the murders had taken place. Preate motioned the court to allow a walk-through inspection, by the jurors, of Corey Slope, the stripping pits and the new house.

Jack Brier considered it a problem to have Joey at the viewing of the crime scenes. With these thoughts in mind, Brier said, "Your Honor, with respect to the defendant, I mean I don't want these jurors seeing him in handcuffs." A deputy sheriff chimed into the conversation, stating, "We didn't intend to put him in handcuffs, Your Honor. What we intend to do is put a belt around him and hold him by it—there's a clip where we put cuffs through, but there won't be no cuff on him at all, just a belt where we hold him in case he starts to run."

Jack Brier thought about the idea of having Joey present at the viewing with sheriff's officers in tow holding him by a belt, and he did not like the idea. "Wait a minute—is it actually a necessity for Joey to be at the view?" Brier asked. Judge Walsh replied, "No, if you don't think you need him there—we just want it on the record, he has a right to be there, but if he doesn't want to be there, there's no question about it."

Jack Brier approached the bench with Joey. Judge Walsh peered over the bench at Joey and addressed him, "Joseph, we want you to be—this is for the record—we want you to know you do have a right to go on this view if you so desire. Your counsel has stated that he doesn't want you to go. Do you go along with that?" Joey addressed the court simply, stating, "Whatever my lawyer has to say, I'll do."

A procession of vehicles snaked its way from the Lackawanna County Courthouse in Scranton for the ride to Old Forge. The convoy passed the Palermo Funeral Home from which the Ziemba children began their final journey to the cemetery, turning right onto Drakes Lane and parking in front of the two-family residence the Ziemba family once called home.

While the jurors disembarked, the state troopers opened the doors and the windows of the new house, which had been vacant since Joey's arrest. High weeds had grown around the Aulisio property. A yellow Ford Pinto sat in the garage bay with its steering wheel missing. Signs on the garage wall greeted the jurors, with one reading, "Vote Robert Aulisio School Director," and the other stating, "I don't get mad I get even."

Judge Walsh entered the new house and began the tour of the crime scenes for the jurors. Walsh had the jurors follow him up the steep and narrow flight of the stairs that led to the upper floor of the new house. Visible on the stairs were what appeared to be stains. A discernible steak of discoloration

Jurors at the viewing of the crime scenes. *From the* Scranton Times-Tribune, *via the Lackawanna County Historical Society.*

traveled from the base of the top stair and down the hallway to a master bedroom as though something had been dragged along the floor.

On the landing, Walsh addressed the jurors, "You will be hearing testimony concerning what was found on the floor in the area, concerning what was found on the floor in the area here. I don't know whether you can see now, but there will be testimony concerning what was found here."

Judge Walsh continued addressing the jurors in the stuffy upstairs of the new house: "You will hear testimony about items that were found connected with the crime on the top step and somewhere in the vicinity of the wall. So, pay particular attention because you will be hearing testimony concerning those areas."

Judge Walsh pointed to the bedroom closet, saying to mesmerized jurors, "You see here the broken off piece of molding, particularly along that area here. Although you can't see it, there is an area with two electric wires coming out of it. You will observe there was no door over there, and one of the items of evidence in the courtroom is of a door, and you will hear testimony concerning that, but that's the area where the door came from."

Judge Walsh had the jurors reenter the four-wheel-drive Blazers for a short ride on the dirt road that snaked up Corey Slope. Once on the top of Corey Slope, Judge Walsh pointed to the area, telling the jurors, "You will recall in the testimony of Mr. and Mrs. LaSota who said they were searching on the following day after the 26th, that Monday, and then came down a path. This is the general area where they found the plastic bag, the carpeting, over around the trees."

Judge Walsh embarked the jurors for a trip up to the strip mining pits. The sheriff's vehicles bearing the jurors proceeded to Drakes Lane, passing the home of the Ziemba children, and turned down Connell Street, retracing the route the killer would have taken to the abandoned strip mining pits.

Judge Walsh started the view by the jury of this area by summarizing what the jurors would be told about the strip mining pit area. "This is our last stop. As to this area here, there are two witnesses who haven't appeared yet who will appear and testify, [one] named Scoda and the other is named Hoover."

Judge Walsh addresses the jury; jurors visit the crime scenes. *From the* Scranton Times-Tribune, *via the Lackawanna County Historical Society.*

THE TRIAL, DAY FOUR

A PROFESSIONAL CRIER?

Jack Brier and Ernie Preate sat opposite each other in Judge Walsh's chamber on the morning of Thursday, May 13, 1982, in a silence that was broken only by an offhand whisper from the judge's staff working in the adjoining room. Preate did not have to be a psychologist to see that Brier had something troubling on his mind.

Judge Walsh entered the chambers and requested from Preate an offer of the witnesses who would be called this day, but before Ernie Preate could utter a word, Brier interjected, "When Mrs. Ziemba was testifying, a member of the District Attorney's staff was sitting in full view of the jury and it seems that Mr. Preate brought out a professional crier to inflame the jury against my client."

"Jack Brier, you have sunk to a new low—you've brought this profession to a new low and I have lost all respect for you as a human being," Preate shouted into Brier's face. "Your Honor, it so happens that a member of my staff was watching the proceeding, Nancy Baldwin, my victim-witness coordinator—let's call her in here and straighten this out right way, I want the Court to see the liar that Jack Brier is," Ernie Preate said in a near shout.

Nancy Baldwin served as the victim-witness coordinator, and it was her job to keep both the victims of a crime and the witnesses at trial informed. Baldwin now stood accused of being a "professional crier" by Jack Brier. Baldwin did not take this accusation meekly, and very soon Brier realized that he had a tiger by the tail. Nancy Baldwin stood more than ready to defend her integrity before Judge Walsh against anyone who dared to question it.

Baldwin advised how the trial was of such great interest to everybody in her office, and most courthouse employees had made their way to the courtroom. When Nancy Baldwin arrived at the courtroom, it so happened that the only seat left vacant was the spot closest to the jury box. "I am just like any other human being," Baldwin told Judge Walsh, adding that "any human would cry during Diane Ziemba's testimony—yes, I was emotional as was about one half of the Courtroom—everyone was in tears." Brier demanded Judge Walsh declare a mistrial, which was immediately denied.

The first witness of the fourth day of trial was the former neighbor, friend and sometime caretaker of Joey Aulisio, Doreen Propersi. She entered the courtroom showing the strain of the events that had transpired since the previous July. Propersi had been just released from the hospital after having been treated for stress.

Doreen testified that in the spring of 1981, she had her boyfriend, Lenny Brown, and Cookie Ziemba retrieve the blue carpet from the basement and had the men lay the carpet out on the lawn to see if it was of any use. Joey Aulisio came walking over to Doreen's property and asked for the blue carpet to use in the log cabin that he was building.

Ernie Preate asked, "This was in April or May of 1981?" Doreen replied, "Yes, and he asked me if he could have the rug; I said, if it was all right with my mom, it was all right with me, he could have the rug. I called my mom and my mom said to give it to Joey and he rolled it up and carried it over to his house."

Preate now showed Doreen Propersi Commonwealth's Exhibit no. 70, the blue carpet found with the bodies of the Ziemba children, and asked if Doreen recognized it. Doreen answered, "It was the whole rug that we gave to him, yes definitely."

Preate continued questioning Doreen Propersi: "The white car, did you ever look inside of it?" "Yes, when he asked me to look at what he had done to the dash, he put a carpet—he fixed it up and he put a carpet on it; his father and brother were working on the car and fixing it up," Doreen responded.

"Can you describe what kind of rug was on the dash?" Preate asked. "To the best of my knowledge it was an off-white shag," Doreen answered.

Ernie Preate now had Doreen stand up and identify the person who had asked her for the blue carpet and who had shown her the white shag carpet on the dashboard of the Plymouth Cricket. Slowly, Doreen rose from the witness stand and pointed with a shacking finger: "Joey Aulisio, he's right there; he is the one that got my blue rug." Joey slowly picked up his glasses from the defense table, placing them back on his face, and then cast a malevolent stare at Propersi.

Preate called Doreen's boyfriend, Lenny Brown, to the witness stand. Brown, a Brooklyn, New York native transplanted to Old Forge, was to give the jury a sense of Joey's knowledge of the use of a shotgun and his conduct during the search for the Ziemba children. "How many times did you go hunting with Joseph?" Preate asked. "Four times," Brown replied.

Preate continued his questioning of Lenny Brown: "Were you able to assess whether or not he knows how to handle that weapon?" Brown replied, "Yes, he was your average hunter, he was really good; you know, he was cautious, always kept the safety on, you know; he was a good shot with it."

Preate questioned Lenny Brown about his interactions with Joey Aulisio on Monday, July 27, 1981, asking, "Do you recall whether or not you had a conversation later on with Joseph?" Preate asked. Brown answered, "Yes, I did, near the partly finished Aulisio home near the driveway."

"What was usual, what was going on there at the time?" Preate asked. "Well, there was fire engines around, State Police and the officers with the K-9 dogs and I waked over to Joey and he was working on his car," Brown replied. "What was he working on?" asked Preate. Brown testified, "He was working on the oil pan because just as I got there, he was pulling the oil pan down. I asked him what happened, and he says somebody sabotaged the oil pan. I asked him, what do you mean they sabotaged it? He told me that somebody hit it with a hammer in the middle of the night."

The testimony of Lenny Brown was followed by another witness from the Empire State. Former New York City Medical Examiner Dr. Dominic DiMaio took the witnesses stand. DiMaio was not an entirely unfamiliar figure in Northeast Pennsylvania. In 1977, he had been called on to conduct a forensic examination of the infamous "Bethany Bones" case, where a skeleton had been found in two garbage bags along a country road near the border of the towns of Bethany and Honesdale in Wayne County, Pennsylvania. When discovered, the "Bethany Bones" were speculated to be the remains of missing one-time Teamsters Union boss Jimmy Hoffa due to all the gold teeth found in the jaw. DiMaio's examination of the "Bethany Bones" settled the question of whether the remains were of Jimmy Hoffa—the skeleton turned out to be that of a woman whose identity has never been discovered.

The career of Dominic DiMaio had not been without controversy, at least according to conspiracy theorists. On November 8, 1965, socialite, reporter and panelist of the popular television program *What's My Line?* Dorothy Kilgallen was found dead in her Manhattan apartment

DiMaio had signed off on Kilgallen's autopsy that the reporter had died of an overdose of alcohol and barbiturates. Conspiracy theorists have long claimed that the autopsy of Kilgallen was a sham, as she was about to write a book about the death of Marilyn Monroe and her involvement with the Kennedy family.

With skull fragments recovered from Corey Slope and at the strip mining pit, DiMaio testified that he was able to reconstruct Cheryl's skull except for a circular hole in the back left side of her head. DiMaio testified that the cause of death for Cheryl Ziemba was a shotgun wound of the left parietal bone, with almost complete avulsion of the scalp.

Testifying regarding the autopsy of Christopher, DiMaio advised that just above the "V" of the little boy's ribcage, the lowermost part of the right chest adjacent to the mid-line, there was a "shotgun perforation measuring one inch in diameter." The wadding from the shotgun shell was found in Christopher's chest.

DiMaio explained to the jury how a shotgun shell is made up of polyethylene wadding, which held the pellets together within the shell. DiMaio opined that the cause of Christopher's death was the massive damage caused to Christopher's heart and lungs. In Dr. DiMaio's expert opinion, the shot that killed Christopher Ziemba came from less than nine feet away. At the request of Preate, Judge Walsh ordered Joey to stand, and Dr. DiMaio then opined that the wound on Christopher, given its angle, was consistent with having come from someone of Joey's height.

Dr. DiMaio next identified photos of the dead children from the autopsy. Several jurors looked quickly at and then looked away from the photos. DiMaio identified shotgun pellets he had removed from the remains of Cheryl Ziemba's head, as well as blue-green glass fragments determined to have come from broken Christmas tree ornaments from the new house's upstairs master bedroom.

Members of the jury grimaced as though in pain when viewing the photos of the Ziemba children. Judge Walsh advised the jurors that he knew that the photos were "unpleasant"; however, the pictures had to be viewed and considered in deliberations.

DiMaio testified that he was able to partially reconstruct Cheryl's skull with the portions of skull found on the Corey Slope culm bank along with a piece of the little girl's cranium that had been found lodged in the stairway of the new house. DiMaio opined that both children were shot from a close range of less than nine feet and that Cheryl was in a crouching position when she was shot.

GIVEN THE NUMBER OF witnesses still to be called, Judge Walsh decided to conduct Saturday testimony. Walsh's decision to extend testimony of a half day on Saturday, May 15, 1982, was further rationalized by the thought of sequestered jurors, unable to watch television, unable to read newspapers and being left in idleness for the duration of the weekend.

Trooper Rovinsky was again called to the witness stand on Saturday morning to bolster the case against Aulisio. Rovinsky testified that the 12-gauge shotgun that the State Police alleged was used by to commit the murders could not be found. Furthermore, Rovinsky admitted in his testimony that no bloody rags, mops or anything else used to clean up the murder scene in the new house had been found.

State Police scientist George Surma was then called to the witness stand. Surma testified that blood antigens found on various pieces of evidence were of the same blood types found in Cheryl and Christopher. Surma would further testify that strands of hair, found in the closet of the master bedroom

Sketch: Trooper Rovinsky testifies. *From the* Scranton Times-Tribune, *via the Lackawanna County Historical Society.*

of the new house on the Aulisio property, matched all the hair characteristics of the hair of Cheryl Ziemba. In 1981 and 1982, forensic science was not what it is today. DNA testing and identification were still decades away.

On cross-examination of Surma, Jack Brier was able to create doubt for the jury on this Saturday morning in May 1982. Surma was unable to clearly establish the chain of custody of the evidence and how it came to him. Ernie Preate sat at the prosecution table with Mike Jordan and privately fumed. No evidence was lost. However, a clear explanation was missing of how the evidence was brought to Surma and preserved thereafter.

THE TRIAL, WEEK TWO

George Surma from the State Police Crime Lab was back on the witness stand on Monday, May 17, 1982. Surma testified and identified each piece of evidence that he had examined. Preate took special case to ask questions to clarify the chain of custody of each exhibit Surma had tested.

Surma testified that both the blood and hair found in the master bedroom closet of the new house, on the carpets found with the bodies in the strip mine pit and on Corey Slope were consistent with blood of Cheryl and Christopher Ziemba. Surma testified that two fragments of blue/green colored glass removed from the skull of Cheryl Ziemba matched the pieces of broken Christmas ornaments found in the master bedroom closet.

George Surma went on to testify for the entire morning court session. Surma added to his testimony that the fibers, collected by Trooper Rovinsky from the trunk of the Plymouth Cricket, were similar in all characteristics to the pieces of carpet found both on Corey Slope and in the strip mine pit with the bodies of Cheryl and Christopher. Surma further elaborated that human blood was found on a spent 12-gauge shotgun shell found under the bed of Joey Aulisio.

Preate's staff wheeled a blackboard into the courtroom that he used to go through with Surma more than sixty pieces of evidence. Skillfully using the blackboard prop, Preate had Surma identify the origin of each piece of evidence and the chain of custody for each.

Working to repair the damage done during the Saturday court session, Preate had Surma testify further about the blood evidence. Surma testified that blood containing the same H and type O antigens as Cheryl Ziemba's type O blood was found on the inside of the closet door of the master bedroom of the new house.

Surma's testimony took the entire morning. The jurors were escorted out to lunch by the court tipstaffs and then escorted back to the courthouse. As the jurors began to walk into the building, a pickup truck stopped in traffic on Linden Street, and the passenger screamed out to the jurors, "Hang him!"

When court resumed, Jack Brier demanded a mistrial. Joey Aulisio seemed to take no interest in the courtroom proceedings, continuing to stare idly at the floor while, from under the defense table, continuing to wave the middle finger at Ernie Preate and Mike Jordan. Although Joey was not taking things seriously, Judge Walsh found the issue serious enough to put a hold on the trial while he interviewed each juror individually.

One by one, each juror was escorted to the chambers of Judge Walsh. It turned out that the jurors had not heard what was said and advised that the comment would not affect their ability to decide the case. Judge Walsh denied the mistrial motion despite a series of arguments made by an increasingly furious Jack Brier.

FBI SPECIAL AGENT JAMES Corby was Preate's next witness called to the witness stand. Corby testified that two blue particles found after Trooper Rovinsky had vacuumed the closet of the master bedroom of the new house matched particles found in the remains of Cheryl Ziemba's head.

Another FBI agent followed Corby on the witness stand. In his testimony, Agent Ed Burwitz said that his test comparison of the blue carpet found on Corey Slope and at the strip mine pit matched the fibers of blue carpet found in the new house, the trunk of the Plymouth Cricket and the floor of Joey Aulisio's "bunk."

It was the first time Kenny Comcowich had seen his former friend Joey Aulisio since testifying at the preliminary hearing. Comcowich shied away from Joey's stare through his thick glasses when walking to the witness stand. Aulisio adjusted his glasses and continued to stare at Comcowich.

Preate questioned the youth about his friendship with Joey and began an inquiry regarding the events of July 26, 1981. Comcowich described how his mother drove him to Joey's to borrow from a funnel for gasoline. Comcowich testified that he had his mother wait in the car while he went to the door of the new house.

"What happened when you went to the front of the garage door?" Preate asked. "Well, I was standing there, and Joe came out from another room, into the garage," Kenny answered. "Came out from another room, how do you know?" Preate asked. "Because I watched him come out from the other room," Kenny replied.

"Ken, did he open the door?" Preate continued. "No, he didn't," answered Comcowich. "Were you able to talk to him, how?" asked Preate. "One of the windows was broken out and there was a screen, like a fence, over it," Kenny replied.

Kenny testified regarding Joey's appearance: "Well, he had no shirt on, and he had a pair of pants on. His top was wet, as if he were sweating. I asked him if I could use the funnel, and I asked him where it was, and he said it's around somewhere. I started looking for the funnel outside of the garage. There was a white hood to a Pinto, and I picked it up and looked under there. Well, there was a red spot underneath the hood. It was like a reddish black spot. It was on the concrete slab that was the driveway going into the garage. It was about two to three feet away from the garage door."

"Did anybody say anything when you lifted the hood?" asked Preate. "J.R. Davis asked Joe who got cut, and Joe said, 'I did.'"

Preate asked Kenny, "When was the next time you went to the Aulisio home?" His reply was, "Monday, the 27th, at about a quarter after 5:00 P.M." "What did you go there for?" Comcowich drew a breath, looking away from his former friend, and answered, "A carburetor."

Kenny Comcowich testified that on July 27, 1981, Joey was sitting in his car with an adult named "Franko" and was smoking pot in the car, with Kenny telling Joey to hide the pipe because his mother was waiting on the street in her car. Comcowich told the jury that Joey told him he would look around for a carburetor, and if he could not find one, he would try to steal one from a station wagon parked up the street. Kenny further told the jury that he, along with Joey, then entered the new house on the Aulisio property to look to see if Joey had a carburetor.

Ernie Preate now asked Kenny, "Did you have a conversation with him at that time?" Watching Joey Aulisio sitting at the defense table out of the corner of his eye, Comcowich answered. "I just—I said, I think you did it." Preate pressed Kenny for further detail, asking, "Referring to what?" Kenny answered, "The Ziemba children." Preate continued, "And he didn't answer you?" Kenny Comcowich answered, "No."

J.R. DAVIS WAS THE next witness. Ernie Preate was suspicious of Davis's ability to tell the truth. Mike Jordan ordered plainclothes state troopers to tail Davis during the lunch break. Sure, enough Davis and his mother were spotted having lunch with Joey Aulisio's mother, Claire.

"Now, do you know Joseph Aulisio, and are you friends with him?" Preate asked the skinny teenager. "Yes," Davis answered. "In fact, you still communicate with him in the jail by writing him letters, don't you?" Preate continued. "Yes," said Davis.

Laying the foundation for the jury of how close J.R. Davis still was to the Aulisio family, Preate asked, "And you just had lunch with his mother?" J.R. Davis meekly replied, "Yes." "Did you discuss this case and your testimony with Mrs. Aulisio?" Preate continue. "I don't remember," a trembling Davis replied. "Sure, you don't," Preate said, looking the teenager square in the eyes.

"And when you were over at the unfinished house, late afternoon on Sunday, what transpired?" Preate asked. "We seen a little spot of blood," J.R. answered. "How did you get to see the little spot of blood," asked Preate. "I just noticed it, it was sticking out from underneath the hood, the white hood on the ground of the Pinto," Davis replied.

"What was the nature of discussion that was going on at the time?" Preate inquired. "I said who got cut and Joey said he did," Davis replied. Preate now noticed the hesitancy in his answers and took note of an attempt to be evasive in answers to his questions. Clearly, the teenager was trying to demonstrate continued loyalty to his friend.

In follow-up questioning centering on the Plymouth Cricket, Preate conducted a colloquy with J.R. Davis. "Did you notice anything on the dashboard of it?" Davis hesitated again and answered, "He put on a white shag rug."

"Had he taken that white rug off the dashboard of his car before July 26, 1981?" asked Preate. "Yes, I think he put it in the garage," Davis answered.

Jack Brier in his cross-examination of J.R. Davis worked to demonstrate that Joey had been involved in the search for the children the entire night of July 26, 1981, to 6:00 a.m. the morning of July 27, 1981, leaving no time for Aulisio to dump debris from the crime scene on Corey Slope. Davis had testified that during the night of searching, there were some points of time when he was not with Joey,

Asking about Corey Slope, with the aim to prove that all the neighborhood teenagers were familiar with it, Brier asked Davis, "You played up on Corey Slope sometimes with Joe and sometimes without Joe?" with J.R. quickly replying, "Yes." "Is there a kid in the neighborhood that didn't play on

Sketch: J.R. Davis testifies. *From the* Scranton Times-Tribune, *via the Lackawanna County Historical Society.*

Corey Slope outside the little shavers?" continued Jack Brier. "Even the little kids know it," Davis answered.

Davis testified under questioning by Jack Brier that Kenny Comcowich had not been to the Aulisio property on either Sunday, July 26, 1981, or Monday, July 27, 1981. Therefore, Kenny Comcowich could not have seen bloodstains on the Aulisio property, Davis concluded with a self-satisfied smirk.

Following Jack Brier's cross-examination of Davis, the opportunity to tie up loose ends was taken by Ernie Preate, who elected to conduct what is called "redirect examination." "You don't know what Joseph was doing during that time that you weren't with him?" asked Preate. "No," Davis tersely replied.

Kenny Comcowich's mother, Dolores, was the last witness called on Wednesday, May 19, 1982. Mrs. Comcowich testified of driving Kenny to the Aulisios' new house on both July 26, 1981, and July 27, 1981, and waiting for her son as he borrowed tools from Joey Aulisio. Preate used Dolores Comcowich's testimony to refute any claim by J.R. Davis that Kenny was not on the property on either July 26, 1981, or July 27, 1981.

More witnesses were expected to be called to testify on May 19, 1982. However, a bomb scare had been called into the court, and Judge Walsh decided that the court proceedings should end for the day.

THE EYEWITNESSES

For the tenth day of the trial, Thursday, May 20, 1982, Tom Scoda was called to the witness stand. As Scoda took the witness stand, powerful thunderstorms began to roll through Scranton. Sounds of hard rain hitting the sides of the courthouse and then thunderclaps echoed in the courtroom.

Tom Scoda testified about getting out of work on Sunday afternoon, July 26, 1981, and driving with Alan Hoover to load up brush to be dumped in the old strip mining pits in the mountains south of Old Forge. He testified that he and Hoover were just about done with their task of dumping brush when they heard a loud noise of a vehicle's engine coming up the road. Scoda added that he was surprised when it turned out to be a small white car, and being interested in cars, he took a good look at the car, as the front end seemed to him to be unique. Scoda testified that the driver seemed to be a young kid with bushy hair and glasses.

Scoda testified that he was able to get "very good look" at the driver of the white car. Tom Scoda said the car had come up the road between 4:45 p.m. and 5:00 p.m. on July 26. Tom Scoda then testified that what really stood out about the driver of the white car were "his wide frame glasses."

After first positively identifying a picture of the white Cricket as the vehicle he saw up on the mountain, upon Preate's request, Tom Scoda stood up in the courtroom and pointed out Joey Aulisio as the person he saw driving up on the mountain road in the small white car on July 26, 1981. Just then there was a loud crack of thunder. The lights in the courtroom flickered. "Are you positive, Tom?" Preate asked. "Yes, sir," Scoda replied. "Any doubt in your mind?" "No sir," answered Scoda.

Following the testimony of Tom Scoda, Robert Colburn was called to the witness stand. Colburn testified that on the morning of Monday, July 27, 1981, he went over to the Aulisio property to find Joey working on the Plymouth Cricket in his driveway. Colburn noted that when he questioned Joey regarding the problem with the car, Joey told him that "some firemen had punctured the oil pan with a screwdriver." Colburn then told the jury that when he looked at the oil pan, it looked as though there was a crease in it and that small pieces of rocks were embedded in the metal.

Myron Jenkins next testified that Joey had told him, on Monday, July 27, 1981, that the oil pan of the Plymouth Cricket had been broken by Bobby Aulisio. Jenkins further added in his testimony that he had noticed a car hood from a Ford Pinto in the driveway of the new house on the Aulisio property and that when he moved the hood, a large reddish-black stain was revealed.

Jenkins testified that when he, Bobby Aulisio and Colburn were looking for tools on the afternoon of July 28, 1981, they went to the new house, found the door was locked and heard noises from inside. Joey eventually came to the back master bedroom window and yelled down that he would be back down in a minute, Jenkins testified.

Old Forge gas station owner Mike Schuback followed Colburn and Jenkins on the witness stand. Schuback testified that on the afternoon of Tuesday, July 28, 1981, he was depressed over the murders of his friend's children and had not intended to do any work when Bob Aulisio walked into his shop. Bob Aulisio, Schuback noted, brought in an oil pan from a car to be repaired. Believing that keeping busy would keep his mind off the murders, Schuback testified that he agreed to repair the oil pan.

Schuback testified that the oil pan given to him by Bob Aulisio looked as though it had been scraped on rocks. He opined that the damage to the oil pan could not have been done by a screwdriver, nor did the damage look like it was the result of running over a car ramp.

After Schuback testified, Judge Walsh called both Brier and Preate into his chambers once again. Walsh informed legal counsel that more bomb threats had been called into the courthouse and that testimony would cease for the day.

BOBBY AULISIO HAD TRIED to avoid being present for his brother's murder trial since the first day. He fidgeted in the witness stand with a worried look. In Bobby's hand was the subpoena compelling him to testify.

Preate focused his direct examination questions on where Bobby was on the afternoon of July 26, 1981. Bobby had a pained expression while testifying, as though knowing that although he was exonerating himself, he was now making it harder for Joey.

Preate had Bobby admit to the court that he could have been at the softball game as late as 6:00 p.m. Preate had Bobby read his statement to the State Police to the jurors confirming the testimony of Myron Jenkins that on Tuesday, July 28, 1981, Jenkins and Bobby heard noises coming from inside the new house and that Joey had been inside the house.

Alan Hoover was called to the witness stand. Mirroring the testimony of Tom Scoda from the day before, Hoover told the jury of the appearance of a small white car that was driving very fast considering the condition of the road. As his friend Tom Scoda had done in his testimony the day prior, Hoover stood up and identified Joey Aulisio as the boy he saw driving the white car on July 26, 1981.

Trooper Gerald Gaetano was called by Preate to the witness stand. Gaetano's testimony seemed the product of an organized and methodical thought process, setting forth the events that occurred following the entry by the State Police into the Aulisio trailer. Gaetano spoke of moving the Aulisios from the trailer into the State Police cruisers in Old Forge and of taking all three—Bob, Bobby and Joey—to the Dunmore State Police Barracks for questioning.

Top: Bob and Bobby Aulisio walk out of the courthouse. *From the* Scranton Times-Tribune, *via the Lackawanna County Historical Society.*

Bottom: Sketch: Alan Hoover testifies. *From the* Scranton Times-Tribune, *via the Lackawanna County Historical Society.*

Preate next had Gaetano testify regarding Joey's near confession. Gaetano said that upon his mother Claire's urging, Joey suddenly burst into tears and between his sobs said, "All right, I was framed. It was about 6 p.m. Sunday night. I went into the house. There was blood all over the place. I figured I better clean it up before I get in trouble. My father found a shotgun in the closet."

Top: Sketch: Jack Brier cross-examines Trooper Gaetano. *From the* Scranton Times-Tribune, *via the Lackawanna County Historical Society.*

Bottom: Claire Aulisio walking out of courthouse. *From the* Scranton Times-Tribune, *via the Lackawanna County Historical Society.*

Gaetano testified that Joey looked directly at him with a strange look on his face with his eyes opening very wide, saying to the trooper, "Oh God. It was fucking disgusting. I'll never forget it. When I walked into that room it was like a horror movie. Somebody tried to frame me. But I caught on. I caught on."

Brier also focused his cross-examination on the scene outside the Aulisio trailer in Old Forge on the night of July 29, 1981, as the State Police escorted Joey from the Aulisio family trailer. When asked about the mood of the crowd and the tension surrounding escorting the Aulisios from the trailer, Jack Brier got Trooper Gaetano to admit that "it wasn't good."

Lieutenant Mike Jordan left his seat at the counsel table where he had been seated next to Preate as the first witness of the second successive Saturday court session. Joey Aulisio placed his glasses on his face before Jack Brier could stop him. Aulisio gave a long glare at Jordan, conveying an impression of a special, deep hatred. Joey blurted out "scumbag" as Jordan sat down in the witness stand.

Answering Ernie Preate's questions, Jordan walked the jurors through the entire investigation of the Ziemba murders, starting when he observed the pieces of human skull and brain matter on Corey Slope, turning a missing children investigation into the search for a murderer. Ernie Preate wanted Jordan's testimony to be one of the last things that the jurors heard of the Commonwealth's case. The jurors sat forward in their chairs listening to Jordan testify and nodding their heads, as though Lieutenant Mike Jordan brought together all the things that they had heard from the previous witnesses.

BOB AULISIO TESTIFIES
FOR THE PROSECUTION

A nervous Bob Aulisio slowly walked to the witness stand, his steps echoing in the hushed courtroom. It seemed to Mike Jordan that the elder Aulisio had lost the swagger and bravado he had demonstrated in the hallways of the courthouse.

Preate's purpose for having Bob Aulisio testify was limited. Preate wanted the elder Aulisio to refute Joey's claim to the State Police that his father had found the 12-gauge shotgun in a closet in the new house on the night of the

Sketch: Bob, Bobby and Claire Aulisio at trial. *From the* Scranton Times-Tribune, *via the Lackawanna County Historical Society.*

murders. Bob Aulisio denied that he ever had found the missing shotgun in the closet.

Bob admitted that he did ask Bobby to look for Joey in the new house on Tuesday, July 28, 1981. Bob also admitted that when Bobby and Myron Jenkins went to look for Joey, noise was heard coming from the new house.

The final witness to be called against Joey Aulisio was James Rinaldi, the physician's assistant at the Lackawanna County Jail, who testified that upon examining Joey Aulisio in the early morning hours of July 30, 1981, he found no cuts on the teenager. Thus the jury was left considering how Joey Aulisio claimed to friends on the evening of July 26, 1981, that the pools of blood on the garage floor of the new house and on the driveway in front of the structure came from him being cut.

In a strategic move, Preate indicated to the court that he would now be moving for all 138 exhibits thus far presented in the Commonwealth's case to be admitted into evidence. Judge Walsh ruled that Preate, through witness testimony, had clearly established the chain of custody of the blood evidence. At 10:54 a.m. on Saturday, May 22, 1982, after twelve days of testimony, the Commonwealth of Pennsylvania rested its case against Joey Aulisio.

THE LAST MONDAY OF MAY

J ack Brier stood at the defense table and glanced at the courtroom clock showing that it was now 10:04 a.m. on Monday, May 24, 1982. Clearing his throat, Brier began his opening statement.

Mindful that he had no intention of calling Joey to the witness stand, Brier reminded the jurors, "Joseph has no obligation to take the stand here and testify. A very good reason for it. He doesn't even have to present any defense, and at this point, we could close because Joseph doesn't have the burden here."

Brier spoke to the jury regarding whether Joey's statement to the State Police on July 29, 1981, was voluntary. Brier told the jurors that Joey's guidance counselor would testify that his IQ was in the range of 81 to 89 and that her dealings with the teenager were proof that he would not have understood the meaning of the words of his waiver of the right against self-incrimination. Brier next pointed out to the jury that if they found Joey's statement to the State Police was not voluntary, then "you will have to wipe it from your mind."

Wrapping up his opening statement to the jury, Brier concluded, "I will present a number of other witnesses, hopefully their testimony will be very short and to the point, succinct. I will let the witnesses tell you what they are going to say. You'll hear it from them; not me, so there is no mistake." Exhaling louder than he intended, Brier glanced at his watch, showing that he had been speaking for thirty-nine minutes.

Paul Kuzara testified that he did not arrive home until early evening on July 26, 1981. Kuzara told the jurors that at approximately 9:00 p.m., after being informed by Bob Aulisio that the Ziemba children were missing, he suggested they should check the new house on the Aulisio property. Utilizing Kuzara's lantern, the two men checked the house, which was normally unlocked, and did not find any sign of the children.

Kuzara admitted on cross-examination that he had no idea what happened in the neighborhood up to the time he arrived home on July 26, 1981. "You were looking for live, stand-up kids weren't you," Preate queried Kuzara. "Yes," Kuzara replied. Preate asked, "You didn't go into the closets of the house, did you?" Kuzara admitted, "No, we didn't."

Kuzara's testimony was followed with Jack Brier calling Old Forge police patrolman Henry Wylam to the witness stand. Wylam testified that during the early morning hours of July 27, 1981, he along with the uncles of the Ziemba children—Leonard Ziemba, Robert Ziemba and Joseph Ziemba—searched the new house on the Aulisio property. The police officer testified that the door to the new house was not locked when they entered the building and that the men had gone as far into the structure as the steps leading to the upstairs, yelling for the children.

Brier tried to elicit in Wylam's testimony the idea that Joey was blamed by most people in the neighborhood for all criminal activity there. This attempt by Brier brought an immediate objection to Judge Walsh by Preate, as Jack Brier had failed to mention this claim in his opening statement.

Sternly looking down from the bench, Walsh said to Jack Brier, "Mr. Brier, once you go into this, you open yourself up for cross-examination." "Oh my God," Ernie Preate yelled out to Judge Walsh, "you cannot allow this in; he didn't mention it in his opening statement."

Jack Brier looked smugly at Preate and said, "I don't have to." Judge Walsh had enough of it all, his patience clearly worn thin, and looked down toward Brier and ruled, "You are opening up a Pandora's Box, Mr. Brier, and I will only allow instances in which Patrolman Wylam has actual personal knowledge of."

Jack Brier continued Wylam's testimony, eliciting various instances in the trailer park neighborhood when Joey had been accused of stealing bicycles that were unsubstantiated. Wylam further referred to the incident on Corey Slope where Joey had thrown rocks at Little Leaguers on the ballfield.

Preate then cross-examined Wylam, who admitted that while in the new house the bedrooms and the closets were not searched. Patrolman Wylam also admitted that while in the new house he was not looking for bloodstains but rather was searching for live children. Preate delved into the Corey Slope culm bank incident where Joey had attacked Little League ballplayers. Wylam testified that one boy had been hit in the leg with a tractor tire that was rolled down Corey Slope to the ballfield and that another player had been injured by rocks thrown by Joey.

Brier called Maria Szymanski as a witness. Szymanski had been Joey's guidance counselor at Old Forge High School since September 1979 and his teacher in grammar school during the fourth grade. Szymanski testified that Joey Aulisio's IQ as tested in April 1981 was 81.

Preate quietly sat writing on his yellow note pad, preparing for cross-examination. "A learning program has a lot to do with interest, does it not, in one's school subject, in other words, isn't it a function of learning that you are actively interested and attend school and are interest in the subjects you are taking?" Preate asked Szymanski. The guidance counselor seemed taken aback by the question and gave an affirmative grunt of "mmm."

Preate continued, "You had taught Joey in the fourth grade, and he didn't have a learning problem at that time, did he?" Taking a moment to adjust her seating position in the witness stand, the guidance counselor answered, "If you are not in school it is difficult to learn, and Joey had a high rate of absences from 1979 onwards."

"And so, by the early part of 1980, there was a marked increase in Joey's absenteeism rate, isn't that true?" Preate inquired. "In 1980 Joseph Aulisio was out from school a total of thirty-eight times," Szymanski answered.

Pressing the guidance counselor on the issue of Aulisio's truancy, Preate continued his line of questioning: "In the 1981 school year Joseph had ninety-one absences, isn't that correct?" "Yes," replied Szymanski. "Well, it is pretty difficult to learn isn't it, if you miss ninety-one days of school out of the school year?" Preate asked. "Well, it certainly wouldn't help," Szymanski answered.

There existed a State Police report from the Monday after Joey's arrest that Joe Lilli claimed to have seen the Ziemba children at 4:30 p.m. on Sunday, July 26, 1981. It was the hope of Jack Brier that he could create an inference to the jury that if the children had been seen by Lilli on the day of the murders at 4:30 p.m., Joey would have not had enough time to murder the children, drive up the mountain and hide the bodies by 5:30 p.m. Joe Lilli, a musician by profession, had suffered three strokes since the murders. It was entirely conceivable that Joe Lilli's memory was clouded by the strokes and he might blurt out testimony highly unfavorable to Aulisio. Knowing the risks, Jack Brier decided to call Joe Lilli to the witness stand.

The gamble on Joe Lilli as a witness did not go well. "Do you recall July 26—" Brier began to ask. Joe Lilli interrupted Brier and blurted out, "Yes, I recall last year I saw the Ziemba children from 3:00 p.m. to 3:30 p.m., the children had been playing in the sandbox that I had for my little girl." The timeframe Jack Brier had been attempting to establish had just been shattered.

Brier tried to rehabilitate his timeline with further questions, which did not go as planned. "Now sometime that day did you leave for Snack & Putt restaurant?" asked Brier. "Between 4:15 and 4:30 I think I left but I am not positive," Lilli answered.

"The next day—" Brier attempted to ask, but Ernie Preate rose to his feet shouting an objection and then requested Judge Walsh allow Joe Lilli to testify in his own words. Walsh sustained the objection.

Brier tried again. "All right Mr. Lilli, when you left for Snack and Putt did you see the Ziemba children?" Shaking, Joe Lilli stammered, "I can't remember, I honestly can't remember seeing them," then adding, "They were always playing around that property, they could have gone there before I left, I don't remember, I'm sorry I can't remember." Lilli began to openly weep on the witness stand. Jurors fidgeted uncomfortably in their seats.

Jack Brier tried to save the situation, asking Joe Lilli, "Did some state troopers and the district attorney take you down to the District Attorney's Office this morning?" Joe Lilli continued crying and between sobs answered, "I can't understand what you are saying."

Jack Brier made yet another attempt to get through to Joe Lilli, asking, "On July 27, did you state to the State Troopers that you heard the Ziemba boy crying?" Lilli stammered, "Brian?—I'm sorry I don't understand what you mean.…I don't understand what you mean."

Ernie Preate continued his objection to Judge Walsh: "Your Honor, excuse me, I think we have gone far enough, the man indicated that on two occasions he couldn't remember." Jack Brier turned and looked toward Joe Lilli on the witness stand and said, "Ok, alright, I have no further questions."

Preate knew Joe Lilli from growing up in Old Forge and tried to make cross-examination of the man as easy as possible. Lilli attempted to walk away from the witness stand, and Preate rose from his counsel table and said, "Joe, I'm not finished here Joe, Joe just sit down there OK?" Preate gently moved Lilli back to the witness stand and asked, "Joe, how many strokes have you had?" He answered, "Three, they have drilled a hole in my head now." In a soft voice, Preate asked, "Joe, do you know who I am?" Joe Lilli managed to blurt out, "Ernie Preate, I know you." Preate nodded to Joe Lilli and said, "Joe, I don't have any other questions, why don't we just go home, OK?" Ernie Preate walked up to the witness stand and led Joe Lilli out of the courtroom.

Brier attempted to call as a witness State Trooper Chester Kuklewicz, whom Brier claimed took a statement from Joe Lilli in which Lilli claimed to have seen the Ziemba children by his trailer on the day they disappeared at 4:30 p.m. There was an immediate objection by Ernie Preate, and both he and Jack Brier approached Judge Walsh's bench for a sidebar conference. "The Trooper will testify for the sole purpose of whether he spoke to Mr. Lilli, Mr. Lilli had stated to the Trooper on July 26, 1981, he saw the children at 4:30 PM," said Brier.

"This is an attempt to get in the back door something he could not establish directly; he is trying to impeach his own witness," Preate told Judge Walsh. Brier shot right back, "I'm going to plead surprise, because this morning Mr. Lilli stated the last time, he saw the children was between 4:00 and 4:30, and I know that is prior to the DA's office woodshedding my witness."

Preate threw a hostile stare in the direction of Jack Brier. "That's not true, that's not true and you know that Mr. Brier—he didn't deny he said it, he said, 'I don't remember,' so how can that be inconsistent and how can you be surprised?" Preate yelled into Brier's face. Continuing, Preate added, "I would tell the court that the first time I spoke to him in the presence of his wife, he told me what he said on the stand."

Judge Walsh interjected, "What you are trying to do is get testimony in which he says he doesn't remember, you're trying to get impositive testimony, not impeaching testimony."

Brier responded to Judge Walsh, "I want an independent—before Mr. Lilli leaves here and his wife, I want an independent hearing in chamber on what happened in the District Attorney's office this morning. Preate says that there was nothing improper done in the office and I say there was!"

Ernie Preate came right back at Brier, "As a matter of fact, you better prove that there is nothing to indicate on the record that we have influenced his testimony and from what he told me Brier wants me to say 4:30 and he's going to be mad if I can't say 4:30." Now eye to eye with Jack Brier at Judge Walsh's bench, in full view of the jury, Preate said, "You're the one that tried to influence him not me."

Preate looked around the courtroom and noticed that the jury was mesmerized at what was transpiring. Lowering his voice, Preate said, "Your Honor, let's do this in chambers, this is getting obnoxious, up here it looks terrible to the jury, I mean, if we had some cooperation with the defense counsel that he'd do this at lunch time, but he won't tell anyone anything." "Not after you started woodshedding my witnesses," Jack Brier snapped back at Preate.

Judge Walsh had enough of the spectacle going on before him. Walsh ruled that what Jack Brier was attempting to do with the testimony of the state trooper amounted to hearsay impermissible at trial and sustained Preate's objection, ruling that the trooper could not testify.

THE DEFENSE, SECOND DAY

Claire Bohenek was next up to the witness stand. The hostility between Bohenek and her former husband was laced into her testimony, as though she was testifying at a divorce trial rather than her son's murder trial. Bohenek made the accusation that the night of Joey's interrogation, the state troopers had slipped into a group of papers a waiver of rights form at the conclusion of the interview.

Preate's first question to Claire Bohenek was a simple one: "Who is Phyllis Zarra?" With an angry look, Joey's mother replied, "She is the girl that broke up my marriage." Bohenek's reply to Preate's questions about the fight she had in the interrogation room with Bob Aulisio was equally terse, stating that Bob Aulisio called her "a fat cunt" and that he had shouted at her, "Why are you always making me out to be the prick—why are you making me out to be the bastard, it must be nice playing God." Claire Bohenek primly concluded, "That is one person I'll never pretend to be."

Having shaken Bohenek's composure, Preate next attacked her version of what occurred in the interrogation room. Bohenek in her answers to Preate's questions wavered in her claim that she was never told by the state troopers that her son was a suspect in the murders of the Ziemba children.

Concerning Bohenek's claim that the waiver of Constitutional rights form was slipped under other papers by the state troopers, Preate's question almost had the tone of a demand, asking, "Do you mean they tricked you?" "I don't know," replied Joey's mother, adding, "I'm not covering up....I can't change nothing, because that's the truth."

Preate put before Bohenek Trooper Gaetano's notes regarding the interrogation with Joey, which noted her son's words that he was in the new house and cleaned up the bloody carnage of the murders and asked if she had any doubt that her son voluntarily made the statement. Bohenek admitted that the statement was voluntarily made by Joey, meekly objecting that she did not remember her son saying anything about a 12-gauge shotgun.

Preate pounced on the admission. "Why didn't you tell the Troopers to correct the statement?" Preate demanded. "I didn't remember it was left out just 'til now," came in reply in a less than self-assured voice.

"You never even told it to Mr. Brier?" Preate shouted at Bohenek, who now meekly agreed about her claimed discrepancy in the state trooper's notes. Jack Brier rose from his seat at counsel table and blurted out, "Don't you remember telling me that?" Judge Walsh admonished Brier, instructing the jury to ignore his comment.

Jack Brier followed up the testimony of Claire Bohenek with photographer Bruno Gallagher, who had been retained by Jack Brier to take pictures from the former home of the Ziemba family on Drakes Lane toward the Aulisio property. Brier wanted to prove that it was not possible for Diane Ziemba to have seen Joey leading Cheryl and Christopher into the new house from the windows of her home.

There were constant interruptions in Gallagher's testimony by objections from Preate to admission of the photographer's testimony for the jury to consider. As Gallagher testified to the pictures he had taken, Ernie Preate thumbed through the photographs that were passed to him from the defense table. Jack Brier stood up in front of the jury, looked at Preate and yelled, "You put one of those pictures into your pocket, didn't you?!" Preate rose to his feet and got nose to nose with Brier before Judge Walsh could intercede. Picking a pencil out of his jacket pocket, Preate threw it onto the defense table and yelled into Brier's face, "I just happened to put a pencil into my pocket." Brier's face was flushed.

It was Preate's turn to question Gallagher on cross-examination, asking the photographer, "Were you there on July 26, 1981?" "No, I wasn't," replied to Gallagher. Preate followed up his first question to the photographer with, "So you don't know what it looked like on July 26, 1981?" Gallagher replied, "No, I don't."

Following a short pause in the trial, Jack Brier called Bob Aulisio to the witness stand. Brier brought Bob through a narrative of his day on July 26, 1981. Bob testified that he woke up around 10:00 a.m. and went to the store to pick up something for the boys to have for lunch. Following lunch, Bob testified that Bobby left for a softball game.

Bob testified that the white Plymouth Cricket was parked on Seaman Lane at 5:30 p.m. in the same spot that he had left the car the night before and that the ground underneath the car was dry, meaning, according to Bob, it had not been moved. Bob further testified that he asked Joey if Bobby was back from the softball game yet, and he was informed Bobby had not yet returned.

Bob testified that he told Joey he was taking the Cricket up to the ballfield to go get Bobby when Joey told him that the oil pan on the car was "busted" and he could not use the car. However, Bob testified that he used the car anyway and drove up the White-Eagle Firehouse, where Bobby was playing softball, and found his eldest son just leaving the ballgame.

Bob Aulisio told how on Tuesday, July 28, 1981, he brought the oil pan of the Cricket to Schuback's Garage for repairs, it would require welding. Bob testified that there was an inch-and-a-half crease in the oil pan that went across the pan to the drain and that after the repairs were complete, he had brought the pan back to Joey.

The never-ending battle with his former wife came front and center before the jury during his testimony. Bob testified that Trooper Gaetano had come into the room and advised that Joey wanted him present in his interrogation room. He testified that once he entered the room, his former wife, Claire, went into what Bob described as "her routine of blaming me."

Preate then launched into cross-examination. Preate had Bob identify the white shag carpets, and Bob testified that he had removed the carpets from the trailer and that the last he had seen them was in either May or June 1981. Bob also identified the carpet from the dashboard of the Cricket.

Preate questioned Bob Aulisio about the blue carpet, having him identify it as the carpet he had last seen in the hut known by Joey as his "bunk." Preate asked the elder Aulisio, "Is it safe to say that the rug was in the hut during July of 1981?" Bob Aulisio answered, "Very safe."

Preate now read to Bob Aulisio a statement Bob had made to Trooper Walter Carlson: "Joey had the key to the new house and if it was locked, I would have to see him to get into the house, Joey used the house more than anyone else." Bob admitted he made the statement.

Bob Aulisio's girlfriend, Phyllis Zarra, was the last witness on behalf of Joey called by Jack Brier. Claire Bohenek gave an icy stare to Zarra as she walked up to the witness stand. Zarra testified that Bob Aulisio had picked her up in Levittown, where she had been house sitting, on July 27, 1981,

Blood behind the baseboard and on the closet floor. *Lackawanna County District Attorney.*

and during the drive back to Old Forge Bob expressed concern that there was trouble in the neighborhood with the Ziemba children and that he had hoped that people would not blame Joey. Upon arriving home Tuesday evening, Zarra testified that the pair went to dinner, bringing along Bobby and Joey.

Phyllis Zarra further testified that during the dinner, Joey had asked Bob, "Dad, why are you nervous?" To this Zarra stated that Bob replied, "I'm not nervous," to which Joey replied, "Yes you are, I have never seen you act like this." Bob Aulisio replied, according to Zarra, "I don't know what's going on down there [meaning the neighborhood], what happening, and I am a nervous wreck, I just want them to get to the bottom of this." At this point, Zarra testified that Joey blurted out, "Dad, I didn't have anything to do with this, how can you think so?"

Preate briefly called Troopers Walter Carlson and William Padula as rebuttal witnesses. Carlson also testified regarding the night of July 29, 1981, that Joey intentionally broke his glasses while being led into the district justice courtroom for the arraignment.

Trooper Padula testified that during the interview of Joey Aulisio in the interrogation room of the State Police Barracks, both Bob Aulisio and Claire Bohenek were present when Joey was read his Constitutional rights.

As a final rebuttal witness for the Commonwealth, State Police Crime Lab Chemist Surma testified regarding hair samples he received and corrected confusion in his testimony about which hair samples he received from the State Police investigators.

THE CLOSING STATEMENTS

In Pennsylvania, the counsel for the defendant is the first to give a closing statement. Jack Brier strode purposefully up to the jury box and began. "Joseph Aulisio comes into this courtroom presumed innocent until he is proven guilty of the crime beyond a reasonable doubt. Reasonable doubt is sufficient to find Joseph not guilty."

Jack Brier attacked the lack of testing of the blood spot on the driveway pad of the new house. "No testimony, this big blood spot that's outside the door. Do you mean to tell me if a blood spot was there, they wouldn't go down and take a sample of it and send it down and analyze it? Why wouldn't they analyze that? Because it wasn't a blood spot."

Brier stated to the jury, "Now, ladies and gentlemen, I think I should address specifically the issue of kidnapping, I think there is no question that was put to rest when Mrs. Ziemba took the stand. You could take all the legal words you want, but when it comes down to God given common sense—you could talk about whether or not there was consent, you could talk about whether or not there was movement of the children for a substantial period of time, but it all comes down to plain common sense. Mrs. Ziemba would not have indicated she saw them going into the house unless in her mind, she felt there would be no problem if they did, and if that were true."

Brier urged the jury to consider the possibility that the district attorney and the State Police were trying to frame his client: "Now let's take the totality of the circumstances. He is a fifteen year old boy who wasn't prime suspect, at home in his trailer all of sudden, all the floodlights, total crowd around, total turmoil, his father in another car, taken in another car with his brother, and he is escorted by two police officers through a maddening crowd with television cameras glaring, gets to the police station and there is another crowd and taken into a room by himself with two police officers, with all kinds of jeers and sheers shouting when he was leaving that trailer park. You tell me that kid knew what was going on at that point in time? I don't care how intelligent he is, he's not, and the proof was uncontradicted regarding Joseph's status. He could never understand those rights that were read to him, and I think that's obvious."

Brier tried to plant the seed with the jury that Joey's mother and father were too busy bickering between themselves to pay attention to their son's rights during questioning by the State Police. "She walked in there and fought with her ex-husband, and this kid is being questioned relative to a double murder!"

Brier turned his attention to the timeline and continued. "In that period of time between 4:00 p.m., giving their time, I submit to you it was a bit later—than 5:30 p.m., and, really, when you get down to it, it's 6:00 p.m., depending on what approach you take, and that time frame, that Joey had to do this." Brier went through all the steps the killer would have had to take to murder the children and dispose of the evidence. Brier concluded, "A fifteen-year-old kid, 140 pounds, in an hour and a half—in an hour and a half. He couldn't do it. He cannot face the death penalty under flimsy evidence."

Following Jack Brier's closing statement, Ernie Preate stood up and walked past the defense table toward the jury. "You scumbag!" Joey Aulisio yelled out loud as Preate passed him. Ignoring the comment, Ernie Preate stood in front of the jury.

"Justice must be achieved. And no doubt, Cheryl and Christopher Ziemba did not kill themselves. They were murdered. They were murdered on a Sunday in July in a little town down in Old Forge."

Preate laid it all out. "I'll tell you right away what the theory is. At 4:00, Sunday, July 26, 1981, Joseph Aulisio took those two little children from the place where he found them, out in the vicinity of his trailer, and took them over to the unfinished house and he shot them to death with a 12-gauge shotgun. He then wrapped up their bodies, the bloody mess that it was, in those carpets, went out and got in that car, drove it around the garage, threw open the garage door, opened the trunk and put them in. Why was he doing that, wrapping them in carpets, because it was still daylight out and if somebody saw him, or by chance came by, and he was carrying a

Sketch: Jack Brier giving his closing arguments. *From the* Scranton Times-Tribune, *via the Lackawanna County Historical Society.*

bloody pulp of a girl with her head blown off and putting her in the trunk, somebody might get a little bit suspicious, and wrap them up in carpet, the blue carpet and the white carpet, and then even tie dungarees around the head because the brains were still falling out, put them in the trunk, the wrapping of the body of little Christopher in there, put them in there. We are not talking about big kids."

Preate walked back over to the prosecution table and picked up the mangled little shirt of Christopher and held it in front of the jury. "Look at this shirt. This is not a big kid to put in a trunk of a car. He put them in there, closes the garage door, closes the trunk. Two miles is all he has to go. He drives up, drops off their bodies, throws them over the slope, jumps back in the car, speeds down, drives out back down the hill again, past Tom Scoda and Alan Hoover, stops halfway down the hill past them, runs over, grabs a blanket that's over there in the car still bloody, takes it out, throws it out in the weeds, runs back up to Corey Slope, right near his house, drives up. He knows all those areas. He takes the bloody blue carpet and white carpet and those things he cleaned up, scooped up, in a plastic bag and in the carpet. He got them in the trunk of the car, opens the trunk, throws it out in the clearing. Covers it up so it looks like another piece of junk, a pile of junk. The next morning, after J.R. leaves, at 10 of 6 or 5 of 6—it's only a couple of hundred feet to the top of that slope, he runs up there in the half darkness. He only gets part of it covered when the LaSotas come around the bend and he has to run out of there."

Preate walked over to the jury and raised his hand just above his knee and then a little higher to his waist. "One little boy is this high and the little girl was this high. There were two separate shots. Who was killed first? Christopher? Was he killed first? I submit to you he was, that he was killed first, based on the testimony in this case, based on the evidence you heard. You can piece together this case because his body hasn't bled much. His body wasn't covered with Cheryl's blood."

Preate continued. "What happened after that? That little girl was still alive. So, you ever remember what you did when you were a kid when you were afraid something was going to happen to you? What did you do? Maybe you ran and hid in a closet or under a bed. She ran and hid in that closet because she just saw her brother get shot, she knew something was wrong; she knew something just happened and she should be afraid. So, she went and hid in the closet, and the killer stalked her into that closet, and when she was down—the bloodstains on that door are not up at the level of the handle or higher. So, you can infer she was crouched down like this." Preate crouched down on the floor in a ball and stood up again. "Yes, it was f-ing disgusting. Yes, it was like a horror movie." The jury seemed stunned that Preate had just used Joey Aulisio's own words against him.

Preate pressed on. "So, let's assume that Kenny comes in between 5:30 p.m. and 6:00 p.m., in between there. This is the period of time between 3:50 p.m., 4:00 p.m., 5:25 p.m. and 6:00 p.m. is when the murders took place in the unfinished home on the Aulisio property, and the bodies were disposed of, and the defendant returned to the scene to clean it up. Somewhere in this period of time is when Kenny Comcowich and J.R. see the same thing. Kenny said it was Sunday. It had to be Sunday the blood was seen. Now just stop for a second and think about this. This is the spot where two people testified as being the area where the blood was. And both of them, incidentally, said it's under the hood and both of them are friends of the defendant. Now why wasn't the blood there when the police went over on Wednesday or Thursday? Why wasn't it even there on Monday? Did you ever think about that? Why wasn't it there? Think about that in your mind for a minute. It all happened Sunday night into Monday morning. Heavy rain washed it away. Use your common sense."

Preate picked up the oil pan and drew a crude sign over it stating "oil pan" and left it again in front of the jurors on the prosecution's table. "Where does all this evidence come in about the oil pan? 'Cause it indicates—consciousness of guilt. On Monday he tells Lenny Brown someone sabotaged it with a hammer. Those four different stories on the oil pan were told, brought out in this case, because it indicates consciousness of guilt, a cover up to try to explain the busted oil pan."

The consistent theme of Jack Brier's defense had been an insinuation that Bobby Aulisio could possibly be the murderer. Preate now addressed this claim: "Bobby, where is Bobby? Bobby is playing softball. And who tells you he is playing softball from 3:00 o'clock to 6:00 o'clock? Bobby tells you; his own brother took the stand, I called him. Who is the one that asks the father about an alibi? And where he was between 3:00 and 6:00 describes what he was doing. Nobody knows where Joey is at these times except for two people in the world, Tom Scoda and Alan Hoover, up on the mountain."

Preate addressed the near confession Joey Aulisio made on the night of July 29, 1981. Preate was keen to make sure that the jurors knew, and remembered, that Joey's statement contained, in Preate's view, several truths that could only lead to Joey Aulisio as the killer of the Ziemba children: "First one is 6:00 p.m. Sunday night, he was in the new house. We know that. Comcowich already told us from the witness stand." Addressing the second truth, Preate told the jury, "He went in the bedroom to clean it up. You can infer that from the testimony here, and from the fact that the doors were wiped, the walls were wiped, the floor was wiped." Preate continued, "Third, there was blood all over the place. It was fucking disgusting. You can infer from what you heard in the testimony and the evidence that blood was all over the place, on the ceiling, the walls, on the door and behind the baseboard. True?"

Addressing the fourth truth of the statement, Preate continued, "6:00 p.m., Sunday night, the bodies weren't there. True. How can you figure that out, because at 5:00 p.m. he was up in the dump throwing them away. We have witnesses that identified him up there." Regarding the fifth truth of the statement, Preate noted, "Five, I always go there. I always go there, he said. It's in his statement." The sixth truth of Aulisio's statement centered on the

12-gauge shotgun. Preate noted to the jury, "He tells you in the statement, spontaneous utterance that the 12-gauge shotgun, the one that was missing, 12-gauge shotgun. Now the bodies were just discovered. We didn't have Dr. DiMaio to do the autopsy until late in the afternoon that indicated what kind of gauge this was. What wadding he took from Christopher's belly unless he knows that a 12-gauge shotgun was used. This is the truth."

Now centered on the seventh truth of Joseph Aulisio's statement, Preate said, "He cleaned it up. Next, cleaned up. You can infer that's the truth from the testimony you heard from Trooper Rovinsky and what you saw on the door and that wall. You confirm that from what you saw on the floor."

Turning the jury's attention to lies that Joey told in his statement, Preate noted, "My father found the shotgun in the closet. Put the father on the stand. The father says no I never found a shotgun in the new house bedroom closet. That's the father who testified….Second, framed, someone tried to frame me, but I caught on. I caught on. If there is one defense that has been suggested in this case, it's framed. The District Attorney framed him. The State Police framed him. Maybe his brother framed him. Maybe his father framed him—or did it. Question is, first, who is that somebody? Is there any evidence that anybody tried to frame Joseph Aulisio?"

Preate now pointed out the absurdity in the claim that Joey Aulisio was framed. "But more importantly, on the frame theory, you think about this now. That person, unnamed for some unknown reason framing Joey Aulisio has to know that at 4:00 on Sunday the area is going to be deserted. But more important, he has to know when he kills those children the very first person that is going to come to the scene at 6:00 is not going to be anyone else in the neighborhood but Joey Aulisio. He has to be God almighty to predict that. And he has to be God almighty to know when Joey finds the mess up there he is not going to report it to authorities; he is going to sit there, and watch Diane Ziemba cry her heart out during the night and not say one word about it. He has to be able to predict at 4:00 on Sunday afternoon for two and a half days, until the State Police interrogate him and question him, he's going to keep quiet about the whole thing. That's what the framer has to know. Otherwise, it doesn't work. It has no chance. Because if you're out there to frame Joey specifically, then you have to know where Joey is going to be."

Speaking of the intent to kill, Preate picked up the little Superman shirt worn by Christopher Ziemba on the date of his death with a large powder-burned entry wound in the upper right-hand corner. "My god, would anybody wish there was Superman inside of here, that the bullets would bounce off. The pointing of that weapon at that part of the body, you can infer a specific intent to kill. Where is the shotgun? It was gotten rid of like the other evidence that had to be covered up, the bodies thrown on the strippings far away, it's almost impossible to get there. You even saw it for yourselves how rocky it is up there. You have to know your way around to get up there. Thrown up there, that's one scene. Another piece of evidence is dropped off on the way down—a blanket in the woods. The third scene is over on Corey Slope. That's the third scene where evidence was disposed of in this crime, three separate scenes where evidence was disposed of. There are more and we haven't found them but there's got to be more. You know how there's got to be more, because we only got one of little Chris's shoes. There is another one of little Chris's shoes around somewhere in this world. So, there is a fourth scene, maybe more, maybe a fifth we haven't found yet in this case. The very fact we haven't found it doesn't put a hole in our case, because you could infer from the fact we only have one of Chris's shoes, there is some other place that we haven't been able to find."

Standing again in front of the jury, Preate picked up the blue carpet, held it in front of the jurors and picked up the little shoes recovered of Christopher and Cheryl Ziemba. "You know, when I look at the evidence, when I look at the carpet over here, this blue carpet and those shoes, these pieces of clothing here, Cheryl's clothing and the clothing of Christopher, this inanimate object, this little shoe, it means nothing, but at one time this had life. Somebody put their little foot in here. And yes, we throw it around the courtroom, the shoes, and I'm almost afraid to touch the blue carpet. It was on the floor in somebody's home, and somebody stomped on it. There were little pieces of life there in that carpet and I think you could never forget this case; we are all alive here. You know it's easy to do the drama of the courtroom and everything else, but we are talking about two people who had life at one time here, Cheryl and Christopher, filled those shoes, that wore those little shoes. Sometimes we've got to stop and think, and you don't forget why you're here."

Silence enveloped the courtroom. Two jurors were wiping the tears from their eyes. Joey Aulisio sat impassively, staring at the floor. Slowly, Ernie Preate walked back to the prosecution table and sat down.

THE VERDICTS

Court reconvened at 9:15 a.m. on Wednesday, May 26, 1982. A juror had become ill overnight and could no longer serve. The last remaining alternate juror now would take his place.

Judge Walsh started reading his long set of instructions to the jury. Joey Aulisio stared at the floor, turned his head to try to stare down Preate and then turned all the way around and looked directly at Diane Ziemba. Diane found the stare of Joey Aulisio to be unnerving. It was a cold, malicious stare. Diane wondered if this was how Cheryl and Christopher felt during their last moments on Earth, facing a stare that invoked a primal fear of danger.

When Judge Walsh finished speaking, Joey had something to say. Aulisio looked directly at Ernie Preate and said in a voice loud enough for the entire courtroom to hear, "You scumbag."

Preate turned to Mike Jordan and said, "Did you hear what he called me…did you hear what he called me?" Jordan said, "Well, I thought he was calling me it—maybe that was for the both of us."

After being brought back into the courtroom after lunch in his holding cell, Joey Aulisio sat slumped in his chair, stared at the floor and conversed with the sheriff's officers. At 2:58 p.m., the jury returned to the courtroom. Brier knew that this was not good sign.

Judge Walsh looked at the jury's verdict slip and sat silently in contemplation. Walsh warned all those present against making any outbursts. Jack Brier reached across the defense table to hold Joey's hand. Aulisio pulled his hand away. Judge Walsh read the verdict finding Joey Aulisio guilty of two counts of first-degree murder and guilty of two counts of kidnapping.

Sketch: Jurors return with the verdict. *From the* Scranton Times-Tribune, *via the Lackawanna County Historical Society.*

Joey Aulisio stood up, put his right arm into the air with a clinched fist and yelled, "It's party time!" Bob Aulisio glared at Joey and yelled, "Shut up!"

Diane and Cookie Ziemba walked up to the prosecution table and hugged Ernie Preate. Joey, being led out of the courtroom, caught a glimpse of the Ziembas and yelled across the courtroom, "Aren't you going to hug me!?" From the courthouse, Joey Aulisio was brought back to the county jail. Imprisonment, which up to now seemed to Joey like a temporary situation, began to acquire an air of permanency.

A quick meeting at the jail with Jack Brier brought no solace to Joey. If things went wrong with the penalty phase of the trial, Joey Aulisio would be going home in a box. The tough guy routine was a façade. The stares and name calling did not work. Joey Aulisio began to cry.

By the morning of Thursday, May 27, 1982, the bravado and swagger of Joey Aulisio returned. He told Jack Brier that under no circumstances would he testify and beg for his life in front of anybody. Jack Brier himself thought it better that Joey did not testify.

There were not many witnesses for Jack Brier to call on Joey's behalf during the sentencing phase of the trial, not anticipating that Judge Walsh would move the sentencing phase of the trial forward without a hiatus to prepare. Maria Szymanski, Joey's guidance counselor, was called to the witness stand again. Her testimony was brief. Judge Walsh ruled that the jury could consider Szymanski's earlier testimony during the trial for the sentencing phase. Adding to her earlier testimony, Brier asked about Joey's school attendance records. For his last school year, Aulisio was absent ninety-one days from school and was to be left back in the ninth grade.

The next witness called was vice principal of Old Forge High School, Walter Ermolovich. A somber Ermolovich testified regarding Joey's years as a young boy. Ermolovich told the court that Joey had been "helpful, active and obedient" as a child. Joey would always, even at age ten, help his father construct the "new house." Joey would even be on the roof of the home helping his father. When Ermolovich "admonished" Bob Aulisio about having the boy on the roof, Bob replied to his friend, "I'm not too keen on roofs myself, but I can't keep him [Joey] away...he's like a shadow."

Ermolovich testified how the death of Maria Aulisio, Joey's infant sister, had destroyed the Aulisio family. Thereafter, Ermolovich told the court that there was a big difference in Joey's behavior, particularly in school. Joey had never been an outstanding student, but "at least he was holding his own." Joey's marks began to slip, he became more introverted and he was "harder to reach." Joey Aulisio had gone from being a "loyal, obedient and helpful boy" to a "hardened teenager."

William Vitack, an employee of Joey's grandmother, testified but had little to offer, relating how the boy was well behaved and was always quiet. On cross-examination, Preate got Vitack to admit that he had seen no difference in Aulisio's behavior after the death of baby Maria.

The September 1981 testimony of Dr. Gerald Cooke, forensic psychologist, was read to the jurors, with Jack Brier reading the transcript of the questions he had presented to Cooke the previous fall and Brier's assistant counsel, Diane Beamer, reading the answers of Dr. Cooke.

Joey's mother, Claire, came back to the witness stand. Following Maria's death, Joey "went downhill" and went "into his shell." Claire testified that after she left the trailer home in 1978, Joey stayed with his father and that she had only seen Joey about ten times from that point up until the night of her son's arrest.

Bob Aulisio was next called to the stand on Joey's behalf. Jack Brier questioned Bob briefly about Joey's personality changes after the 1978 divorce. Bob described Joey as being "quiet and withdrawn" after 1978. When asked about his relationship with his son, Bob Aulisio replied, "I tried my best" and "I don't think our rapport was the best."

In his closing penalty phase statement, in addition to blaming a society that did not help a fifteen-year-old boy, Jack Brier urged the jurors to consider the "kidnapping" convictions that the jury had rendered against Joey just days before to be only a "technical kidnapping."

Jack Brier touched again on Joey's age, noting to the jurors that he was but a few years older than Cheryl, stating that Aulisio was "obviously is a child in our society." Jack Brier again urged the jurors, "Joseph Aulisio is the product of the breakdown of American Society today—there is no question that if Joseph Aulisio is responsible for the death of Cheryl and Christopher Ziemba, American Society is equally responsible."

Jack Brier concluded, "The kidnapping was totally incidental to the crime and shouldn't even be an aggravating circumstance, but it's here because there was a technical kidnapping." Drained, Jack Brier walked slowly to the defense table. Joey continued to stare at the floor as though uninterested in the outcome of the proceeding.

An angry Ernie Preate rose to his feet to commence his closing argument in favor of the death penalty. In a deeper than usual voice, Preate said, "It is a grave day—I don't mean to underscore that....There was, in the proceeding here just a few moments ago, some argument made about murder and about kidnapping. Well, I am not going to insult your intelligence. That has been decided by you."

Walking slowly back to the counsel table, Preate picked up a photo of Cheryl and Christopher, turned toward the jurors and again began to speak. "American Society pulled the trigger that killed two innocent babies? No. I reject that. Reject it. I don't need that guilt on my shoulders, and I suggest that you don't need that guilt on yours, as members of American society. American Society did not force Joseph Aulisio to kill Cheryl and Christopher Ziemba. He did it himself....Was American Society in that closet that day? Joseph Aulisio, by your verdict, was, and he pointed that gun at that little girl, and he blew her head off, and you could think about when you think about that when you think about whether American Society was standing there pulling that trigger. Where?"

Concluding his argument, Preate said in a resolute voice, "We sit here, we breathe, and we live, we eat, we talk, and we'll go home, and we'll sleep with our families tonight. The two that are in eternal rest, let's not forget—there were lives we are talking about—human beings—lives....When you go out and deliberate, do not be afraid. Do not be afraid of what people might say. Follow your conscience, follow the law, follow the fact and evidence in this case, and you will come in with a just and proper verdict, and you will send a message with that verdict that will give meaning and vitality to your first decision in this case, and you will say to all the world—justice has been done."

Jack Brier again tried to hold Joey's hand as the jurors assembled in the courtroom. Joey pulled his hand away. Judge Walsh looked at the jury verdict sheet, his gaze solemn. The verdict was read: death in the electric chair. A gasp could be heard in the courtroom. Joey was quickly led out of the courtroom by sheriff's officers intent on avoiding any outbursts like had happened after the guilty verdict. As of Friday, May 28, 1982, Joey Aulisio was now the youngest inmate under a death sentence in the United States.

Preate, feeling the physical strain of the past three weeks and the weight of the verdict, found himself unable to get up from the counsel table. Reporters quickly congregated, peppering him with questions. Preate looked up and said, "I feel like I just pushed a button to start a nuclear war."

A reporter from the *New York Times* asked a juror about the verdict. "I hate to say it, but that kid gave up his right to live when he killed those children," the juror replied.

Above: Diane and Cookie Ziemba address the press. *From the* Scranton Times-Tribune, *via the* Lackawanna County Historical Society.

Opposite: Judge James Walsh addresses the press. *From the* Scranton Times-Tribune, *via the* Lackawanna County Historical Society.

Fifteen minutes after the verdict was read, the only two people who remained in the courtroom were Diane and Cookie Ziemba, both softly weeping. Cookie had his arm around Diane, and she held tightly to her husband's free hand. Looking toward the reporters who were attempting to keep a respectful distance, Cookie spoke, "We never expected the death penalty, we expected him to get life." Cookie then added, "The death penalty—it's shocking, I don't know how else to explain it."

Diane Ziemba turned to the reporters and said, "I'm scared, that's how I feel. Aulisio scared me when they led him out of the courtroom. Now I know how my children felt those last few minutes after seeing him stare at me."

Preate, Mike Jordan and the rest of the prosecution team were to meet at Revello's Pizza Restaurant in Old Forge after the verdict. Following dinner, Mike Jordan got up to leave the restaurant, and as he was walking out, he ran directly into Bob Aulisio, who had come to pick up takeout. Stares were exchanged. The saga of the Ziemba murder case was far from over.

AFTERMATH

The trial of Joey Aulisio was followed closely by the media. The death sentence verdict made the Ziemba murders national news. In June 1982, the *New York Times* sent reporter William Robbins to Old Forge to interview Bob Aulisio; his mother, Mary Aulisio, who had paid for the cost of Joey's defense; and family friend Paul Kuzara at Mary's dry cleaning business, all of whom emphatically professed Joey's innocence. Bob Aulisio in his interview with Robbins made no mention of his own suspicions of Joey's involvement in the murders of the Ziemba children.

Robbins noted that Claire Bohenek dwelled mainly on the event she saw as leading up to the murders: Bob Aulisio's affair and the divorce that followed. Claire told the reporter, "It was the father...it was the father's girlfriend that screwed Joey's mind up."

A motion to set aside the jury's verdict and for a stay of execution was dutifully filed by Jack Brier less than ten days after the verdict. A stay issued by Judge Walsh pending a hearing on the motion kept Joey Aulisio for the time being in the Lackawanna County Jail rather than Pennsylvania's death row.

Few inmates in the Lackawanna County Jail wanted anything to do with Joey. Child killers traditionally are looked on in prison society with disdain. Luckily for Joey, he had a protector, friend and mentor in the jail's population: "Chimsey," a large, husky inmate who taught Joey religion for the first time and became a father figure to the teenager. Under the protection of Chimsey, few inmates dared to bother Joey Aulisio.

For the Ziemba family, harassment in the form of phone calls started almost immediately after the death penalty verdict had been rendered. Phone calls came with a teenage voice on the other end of the phone asking for "Chrissy."

By the spring of 1984, Joey Aulisio had been under death sentence for nearly two years without leaving the Lackawanna County Jail. In April 1984, Joey Aulisio became a bridegroom, contractually marrying Laura Hueston. The marriage would also prove to be "snakebitten."

On May 17, 1984, Joey Aulisio was again in Judge Walsh's courtroom to hear a final decision on the motion for a new trial. When asked to comment by the court, Jack Brier said, "No one's listened to me so far so I don't see how saying anything now will do any good." Walsh then read his decision to deny Joey's motion and again sentence Aulisio to death.

Judge Walsh asked Joey whether he had anything to say. Aulisio addressed the court, saying, "I don't care if the whole fucking world is against me."

Thus, on May 17, 1984, Joey Aulisio was led out of Judge Walsh's courtroom escorted by Lackawanna County sheriff's officers Jeff Craig and David Gervasi. Joey was allowed for a moment to receive a hug from his mother and quickly snuck a kiss with Laura Hueston.

Joey's initial destination was Camp Hill Prison near Harrisburg, Pennsylvania, for processing. Aulisio was sullen and silent on the trip to Camp Hill, only speaking briefly when he asked to stop and use the bathroom at a rest area. The silence was awkward as both Craig and Gervasi were used

Joey Aulisio being led to Death Row. *From the* Scranton Times-Tribune, *via the Lackawanna County Historical Society.*

to more talkative prisoners during transports. Passing through Harrisburg, Craig pointed out the state capitol dome, to which Joey only replied a dismissive "Yeah yeah." Joey Aulisio's stay at Camp Hill was brief. He was soon transferred to Pennsylvania's death row at Huntington State Prison.

Many years after being sent to death row, Joey recalled, "I lived in a cell. I was fed in my cell all the time. I'd get out for showers. I think like two or three times a week. And the only time I'd get outside for outdoor, you know, get some air and see the sun would be they chain us up and take us to like a row of dog kennels, a chain link fence. Even across the top they had a gate on it."

Joey's appeal moved forward. Aulisio's exceptionally skilled appellate attorney, Joseph Vullo, was tasked with reading more than three thousand pages of trial transcript, attempting to identify errors Judge Walsh made in his rulings at trial, and cross-referencing in a written argument how the precedence of previous case decisions on appeal compelled the conclusion that both guilty verdicts against Joey should be overturned.

Claire Bohenek, Joey's mother, seemed to stop dwelling on her divorce from Bob Aulisio and directed her energies toward pleading her son's case to anyone who would listen. *Parade* magazine, an insert in many of the Sunday Gannett newspapers throughout the United States, ran an article about juvenile offenders sentenced to death in the United States prominently featuring Joey. Several French and Italian magazines featured stories about Joey's plight and cast doubt on his guilt.

In January 1987, an Italian television station paid for Claire along with Joey's brothers Bobby, Dominick, Patrick and Michael, as well as attorney Joseph Vullo, to fly to Rome and have an audience with the Pope John Paul II. The pope offered prayers for the life of Joey Aulisio.

Local Tunkhannock businessman Jay Niskey raised funds to help Claire pay the costs of Joey's appeal. Niskey provided an interest-free $10,000 loan to help further finance the legal fees and costs of the appeal.

On March 19, 1987, the Pennsylvania Supreme Court had the final word on whether Joey Aulisio would die in the electric chair. The court found that Joey Aulisio's guilt in the murders was overwhelming and upheld the murder convictions. However, in a 5-2 decision, the court overturned Joey's convictions for kidnapping and the death penalty verdict.

The court's decision, written by Justice John Flaherty, found that "the evidence of the appellant's guilt is so strong as to leave no question that guilt has been established beyond a reasonable doubt." Flaherty found that Diane Ziemba, having seen Joey walking Cheryl and Christopher into the new house and not objecting, was tantamount to consent to take the children and therefore a kidnapping conviction could not be sustained.

Court observers noted that when Joey came back before Judge Walsh to be resentenced, two supporters of Joey were conspicuously missing: Joey's wife, Laura, and his brother Bobby. The rumor in Old Forge was that Laura was pregnant with Bobby's child. However, the relationship between Bobby and Hueston did not last. Hueston soon ended the relationship, sought a divorce from Joey, cutting all ties with the Aulisio family, and obtained an "Order of Protection" against Bobby.

In October 1987, after seeing Hueston walking down Main Street in Old Forge, Bobby Aulisio appeared at the front desk of the Old Forge Police Department asking that he be taken into custody before he "killed somebody." The duty officers took Bobby into custody but failed to confiscate Bobby's work boots. An hour later, Bobby Aulisio was found in the holding cell hanging by his own bootlaces.

In the wake of his brother's death, his divorce and the reversal of his death sentence, Joey was far from being in a self-reflective mood. He obstinately refused to accept any responsibility for the Ziemba murders. Joey was equally adamant in refusing all interviews with the press. In response to an inquiry from a writer, Joey's eventual response was short and cryptic: "I just wish to cite the article where Ernie Preate said he was surprised that the jury bought it." No such news article exists.

In 1988, Preate's opportunity to seek higher office came when Pennsylvania Attorney General Leroy Zimmerman declined to seek reelection. Preate won the Republican Party nomination for attorney general and prevailed in the 1988 election.

Diane Ziemba, who rarely if ever discussed the murders of Cheryl and Christopher outside of the confines of the family, held Ernie Preate in such high regard that she agreed to appear in television commercials advocating on behalf of Preate's election as attorney general. Beyond this, Diane never spoke to the media. Diane and Cookie had another child; however, it was hard for the Ziembas not to be overprotective of their youngest child, Jamie, a brother whom Cheryl and Christopher would never know.

Cookie Ziemba, always carrying with him the heartbreak of losing Cheryl and Christopher, passed away on June 22, 2001, at the young age of fifty-four. Residents of Old Forge, upon hearing of Cookie's death, whispered of the Ziemba family being "snakebitten."

In 2007, William Hinton, a North Carolina college art professor, received correspondence from Joey Aulisio requesting Hinton review his artwork.

Intrigued to be receiving a letter from a prisoner proclaiming to be an artist and not knowing what Aulisio was incarcerated for, Hinton wrote back to Joey with an invitation to send the professor a sample of his work.

Two weeks later, Hinton received his first painting from Joey Aulisio painted on the cardboard salvaged from a carton of toilet paper. The first painting sent by Aulisio, of a Pennsylvania mining village, struck Hinton and made him even more curious, as it was signed with the initials "AMD."

Hinton received from Joey Aulisio 130 paintings over a ten-year period. In a letter, Hinton found out from Joey what "AMD" meant on his paintings: the initials stood for the phrase "after Mom died." Joey's mother, Claire, passed away in 2006.

Hinton arranged for the artwork of Joey Aulisio to be displayed at colleges throughout the United States. The art displays further hurt the Ziemba family and outraged those in Pennsylvania law enforcement who knew exactly what Joey was capable of.

RESENTENCING

In 2012, the U.S. Supreme Court ruled in the case of *Miller v. Alabama* that mandatory life sentences without parole for juvenile offenders violated the Constitution's prohibition against "cruel and unusual punishment." In 2017, Joey Aulisio, through his attorney Joseph D'Andrea, petitioned the court for a new hearing for resentencing.

In 1988, during my last semester of law school in Columbus, Ohio, I was working on a research paper on the topic of the death penalty as applied in the United States to juvenile offenders. During my research, I became interested in the case of Donald Frohner, who was executed by the State of Ohio on August 20, 1948, for a carjacking-murder committed at the age of sixteen.

It seemed to me that the forty-year-old case of the execution of Donald Frohner would make for a compelling topic for a true crime novel. I was discussing my interest in the Frohner case with a law school friend from the Scranton area when he mentioned the case of Joey Aulisio.

During the summer of 1988, I was in Scranton for a job interview. Following the interview, I went to lunch with the attorney who interviewed me, and I mentioned the Joey Aulisio murder case. The short lunch turned into an hour-long conversation as my host recounted in detail all he knew about Aulisio and the May 1982 murder trial.

In March 1989, I commenced researching the case of Joey Aulisio with a Sunday afternoon trip to the University of Scranton to pull up articles of the *Scranton Times-Tribune* from the university library's microfilm collection. In the fading light of a March Sunday afternoon, I read from the microfilm collection article after article of what seemed to me one of the most compelling crime stories I had ever read about.

In the twilight of that Sunday evening, I found first the Drakes Lane home where the Ziemba family had lived and then went on to locate the new house on Hard Street where the murders had occurred. My self-guided tour finished with a drive down Connell Street to the entrance for the dirt mountain road that led to the strip mining pits, with the orange glow of the setting sun making for an eerie backdrop.

In April 1989, I decided to walk Drakes Lane and the trailer park area. I was taking pictures of Corey Slope when I sensed the presence of someone standing behind me. I turned around and immediately recognized the face of Bob Aulisio.

I was given a relatively friendly greeting by Bob, and I stated the reason why I was taking pictures of Corey Slope. Bob had me follow him onto his property to discuss his son's case. He was emphatic that his son was innocent of the murders. According to him, Ernie Preate, Judge Walsh, Mike Jordan, the Pennsylvania State Police, Laura Hueston and the Ziemba family were involved in a grand conspiracy against Joey.

While with Bob, I paraphrased what Kenny Comcowich had said to Joey in this same garage on July 27, 1981, that in my opinion Joey was guilty. I looked Bob Aulisio in the eye and said that his son deserved to have died in the electric chair.

The Ziemba home as it appears today. *Brian Kincaid.*

Bob Aulisio's response to me was benign and somewhat melancholy, as he claimed in a sad voice that the jurors brought from Bucks County had been drinking during the trial. Opening a drawer in the garage, Bob handed me a letter from prison in which Joey requested legal research regarding cases in which jurors had drank during the proceedings. Bob then asked me to find the research Joey wanted and send it to him. I advised him that I would as a favor since he spoke to me.

I had the good fortune of interviewing defense attorney Jack Brier at his office in May 1989. I interviewed then attorney general of Pennsylvania Ernie Preate in late October 1989. The interview itself did not go well, as Preate seemed hostile to my inquiry and skeptical of my project.

I kept my word to Bob Aulisio and sent Joey the desired research, along with a note advising that I would like to speak to him about the case. Joey Aulisio sent me a brief note in late February 1990 to my law firm address that read as follows:

> *Dear Brian, I just want to cite the article where Preate, said that he was surprised the jury bought it.*
> *JA.*

I continued my research, visiting Old Forge often and interviewing many of the participants of the search for the Ziemba children. A good number of friendships were developed along the way, particularly with firefighter Stosh Zoltewicz.

Then a further letter came to my home from Joey Aulisio. There was no mistaking the tenor and the threatening nature of the correspondence. The letter, dated May 6, 1993, read as follows:

> *Dear Mr. Kincaid, surprised to hear from me? I seen your name and address somewhere and decided to write to find out the defile, excuse me, book is. It's been several years since you began and I'm wondering when I could expect the unpleasantness it is going to cause my family.*
>
> *When you were doing your research in Scranton, reading all those newspaper stories that saturated the media for months I guess you figured my family would like to read all those lies and farfetched caractor [sic] stories again. If I am mistaken about what you wrote, please write and tell me. Did you use my family's real name? Why couldn't you have written a book like* Cape Fear?

```
Joseph Aulisio
Drawer R, AY-3044
Huntingdon, PA 16652


Brian W. Kincaid
143-A Linn Drive
Verona, NJ 07044

May 6, 1993


Dear Mr. Kincaid:

       Surprised to hear from me ?  I seen your name and address somewhere and

decided to write to find out how the defile, excuse me, book is.  It has been

several years since you began it and I am wondering when I can begin to expect

the unplesantness it is going to cause my family.


       When you were doing research in Scranton, reading all those news paper

stories that saturated the media for months, I guess you figured my family would

like to read all those lies and farfetched caractor stories again.


       If I am mistaken about what you wrote, please write and tell me.  Did

you use my familys real name ?  Why couldn't you have written a book like

CAPE FEAR ?


                                              Very Truly Yours,

                                              Joseph Aulisio
```

Aulisio's death threat to the author. *Brian Kincaid.*

The implications of the letter from Joey Aulisio were clear. Firstly, Joey was still refusing to take any ownership whatsoever for the murders. Second, he had taken the time in prison to look up and research my home address. In 1993, such information was difficult to access.

More disturbing was the blatant threat set forth in Joey's letter. *Cape Fear* was a 1962 movie starring Robert Mitchum and Gregory Peck. The plot of the film involves rapist Max Cady (Mitchum) who, after spending eight years in prison for his crimes, tracks down the lawyer, Sam Bowden (Gregory Peck), who interrupted Cady's rape of a woman in an alley and testified against him at his trial. Cady then proceeds to stalk Bowden's family and attempts to kill Bowden himself.

My entry into politics and winning election as a public official in 1998 did what Joey Aulisio's May 1993 letter could not do. The time constraints of working as an associate in a large law firm, coupled now with politics, made finding time to work on writing a book virtually impossible. The project of writing this book was put on the shelf in 1999.

Many of the parties involved in the Ziemba murder case have passed away. Bob Aulisio passed away in September 2014. Bob's estranged wife, Claire, passed away in 2006.

Judge Walsh passed away on July 26, 2019, thirty-eight years to the day of the murders. Walsh was followed shortly thereafter by Jack Brier on September 26, 2019.

In the 2017 November election, Mark Powell was elected Lackawanna County district attorney. Powell came from a long-standing family of prominent attorneys. At the time of the arrest of Joey Aulisio for the Ziemba murders, Mark Powell was in the summer between his junior and senior years of high school, living but a few miles away from the crime scene.

From the first day that he was in office, Mark Powell clearly understood the gravity of the pending hearing for Joey Aulisio's resentencing. Accordingly, Powell would oppose the resentencing application made by Michael D'Andrea, the new defense attorney for Joey.

D'Andrea argued in his petition for resentencing to Judge Vito Geroulo of the Lackawanna County Court of Common Pleas that Joey Aulisio, having served thirty-seven years, should be eligible immediately for parole. After several delays, so that Aulisio could be examined by psychologists about his suitability for rehabilitation, a hearing was scheduled before Judge Geroulo for December 18, 2019.

On Saturday, December 14, 2019, I received a phone call from Stosh Zoltewicz asking me whether I was aware that there was going to be a

mountain on that long-ago summer morning was made when the group decided to "think like a criminal." Recounting the finding of the bodies, "It looked like they were just thrown there like garbage."

Powell next called several prison guards to recount their encounters with Joey Aulisio during his years of incarceration. Testifying were guards Bryan Sharp, Thomas Potsko, Donald McGill and Walter Stankavage. Although Aulisio was usually a quiet loner in prison, all four guards testified that he would become aggressive with prison staff. Each of the guards testified that Aulisio had threatened them and their families, saying that he would kill them when he got out of jail. Each guard testified that Aulisio, when making his threats, would make the motion of loading a shotgun and then the clicking sound that a shotgun makes.

A prisoner in a jumpsuit and handcuffs was led in the courtroom. The prisoner was Carmen Demark, a low-level drug offender and one-time prison friend of Aulisio's. Demark described his relationship with Joey as "very rocky," advising the court that Aulisio "was not a nice guy."

Demark also testified that when his father passed away in 2017, Joey told him that he hoped Demark's father "had a horrible painful death." Demark spoke of how he and Joey would walk laps on the prison track having a conversation when Aulisio would suddenly threaten his erstwhile friend's children when he was released.

"Your Honor, I'm going to call to the stand Brian Kincaid," Mark Powell said. As I sat in the witness stand, I stared evil in the face, and I was disappointed in what I saw. Joey Aulisio, in his powder blue sweater, was slight in build, wearing thick glasses as he slouched in his seat at the counsel table. I thought of Cheryl and Christopher Ziemba and how Joey must not have seemed like a threat to them.

I testified regarding all my research and the interviews that I had conducted. Laughter broke out in the courtroom when I testified—I had interviewed Ernie Preate and stated based on my interview that I did not like Preate very much. I only realized afterward that Ernie Preate was sitting in the courtroom.

I testified regarding my encounter with Bob Aulisio in March 1989 and how Joey knew that I was trying to write a book. Mark Powell's line of questioning directed my testimony to emphasize that at no time did I provide my home address to Joey Aulisio or his father.

I testified in 1993. The internet was in its infancy, and at the time, it was very difficult to find someone's home address, particularly if the person had an unlisted phone number. Specifically, we had the following exchange:

Mark Powell: "Let's put that in perspective in that timeframe. What was a timeframe where the internet was active and people could do searches to locate home addresses easily?"

Brian Kincaid: "No, not at all. I don't even think I heard much of the internet at all at that point in time. We were still using DOS computers. And we were using them at work. It had been a number of years before we got Windows and we were able to start researching on the internet. So the only place that my address could possibly been—not my home address— but office address would be like in the Martindale and Hubble indexes that, you know, for each state that they have attorneys listed."

Mark Powell: "But again, not your home address?"

Brian Kincaid: "Not my home address."

The district attorney next had me read to the court the letter I received from Aulisio in May 1993. Then came the following exchange:

Mark Powell: "So when inmate Aulisio wrote this personal letter to your home address and referenced Cape Fear, *the movie that terrorized individuals when an inmate was released, how did that make you feel?"*

Brian Kincaid: "I was mortified and scared because you just thought how the heck did this guy find my home address. That was number one.

And number two is that the book project kind of had been inactive at that point. I'd never written Joe Aulisio back. So, it was absolutely shocking that you were thinking about it and saying this guy was stewing over the last few years and all of a sudden decided somehow to find out when he's in Huntington Prison your home address and then write you about the movie Cape Fear. *And the implication you can't—it's not a Disney movie.*

You can't think of anything else than somebody wants to come after you."

My testimony was followed by that of four counselors and vocational teachers of Joey Aulisio at prison: Sherri Stempien, Amy Rogers, Courtney McCarthy and Brenda Van Dine. Aulisio had met with Van Dine, a prison counselor, following incidents of misconduct toward his unit manager in prison. Rather than apologize for his misconduct, Aulisio, red-faced and angry, said to Van Dine, "I want you to give her a warning for me. Don't look at me. Don't talk to me. Don't underestimate me. I am full of rage."

Sherri Stempien, a prison social worker, testified that Joey kept to himself in prison and did not interact very much with other inmates. Stempien testified that as late as 2016, Aulisio denied any guilt related to the Ziemba murders, stating to the social worker, "They can't hold it against me if I don't admit it."

Amy Rodgers ran a Juvenile Lifers Safety Group at prison designed to aid those who had been serving life terms sentenced as juveniles. She testified that Aulisio refused to participate in the group and that in her limited interactions with Joey, he never expressed remorse.

Courtney McCarthy, a Psychological Service Specialist, testified regarding her dealings with Aulisio. She testified that he did not express remorse and told her, "I have a plan, I'm going to get out."

The Ziemba family were represented at the hearing by Tracy Muth, a cousin of Cheryl and Christopher, who read letters to the court from herself, her brother and her cousin Jamie. The letters Muth read outlined how the pain of the murders of Cheryl and Christopher never went away.

Muth spoke of remembering the last time she saw her cousins alive at a church fair following Cheryl and Christopher's return from a trip to New York on July 25, 1981: "I remember them smiling and laughing. We were having a great time. I could remember this. It is a good memory." She spoke of the events of Sunday, July 26, 1981: "The events of the next day changed everything. Cheryl and Chrissy were gone, and things were never going to be the same....I will forever remember the phone call from my Auntie Diane telling us that Cheryl and Chrissy were missing. I could also vividly remember seeing from my grandparents' front porch the lines of people searching for them and those same people calling their names over and over again."

Muth testified how cautious and overprotective her parents were of her growing up after the murder of her cousins, noting for the court, "I didn't understand it then. But I do now. As an adult with children of my own I will admit that I was overprotective as they were growing up." Muth reflected on the void left by the deaths of her cousins and how they were never forgotten by the Ziemba family: "Cheryl and Chris's photo hung on my grandmother's wall for as long as I could remember. I have the very same photo on a frame on my wall....It signifies to me they may be gone but they will never be forgotten."

Joseph Ziemba, brother of Tracy Muth but nine years old at the time of the murders, was serving in the military overseas but was permitted by Judge Geroulo to have his voice heard by means of his sister reading a letter from him to the court. Joseph Ziemba's letter spoke of his childhood memories: "What I do remember was that I would never see Cheryl walking to the front of the class to get her grades and her tests. I would not be able to compare her notes with mine while we were in school. You see, while we were in school, we helped each other. Now, I had no one. As I went through the next school year, I remember everyone treating me different from before like I was some sort of outcast, not in a bad way but in a different way. Each time someone said 'Ziemba' in school I got a look of oh, that's one of the Ziembas. To this day when people hear my last name no matter where I am, they associate me with the incident."

Only one of Joey Aulisio's three surviving brothers, Patrick, was in the courtroom. Patrick was the friendly fellow sitting next to me making small talk. D'Andrea's strategy was to have Patrick paint, in testimony, a picture of the home life endured prior to the murders.

While D'Andrea was able to elicit from Patrick that his father, Bob Aulisio, could be violent and that his dad's affair had "broken" his mother, he denied emphatically that it was a household without love. He testified that after his parents' separation, around Christmas 1978, while Joey was not able to visit his mother, Claire, the younger three Aulisio boys visited with their father often. He testified that Bob could be a "Jekyll and Hyde," but his father could also be loving.

There was a mysterious figure in the courtroom wearing a shawl. When the witness named Lindy Morelli was called, the woman stood up and shuffled slowly to the witness stand. Morelli testified that she was a lay woman in the Carmelite tradition. Morelli advised that she was the director and founder of the Light House in Scranton, a nonprofit ministry designed to help the poor.

Morelli testified that she had first spoken to Joey in 1992 and, from that time forward corresponded with him, spoke by phone and visited him in prison. Morelli said further that she was perhaps the only person Joey Aulisio trusted save for his brother Patrick.

Morelli testified that in 1992, Joey told her he "had involvement" with the murders of the Ziemba children. Whispers filled the courtroom, as many of those present in court had been following the case throughout the years and knew that it was only recently that Joey Aulisio admitted to the murders. It occurred to me that when he had written his "Cape Fear" letter to me in 1993, Joey Aulisio had already admitted to Lindy Morelli that he killed the Ziemba children.

Low but audible gasps filled the courtroom when Morelli testified that Joey felt "very trapped and misunderstood." "I wonder how trapped Cheryl and Christopher felt," was whispered in the back of the courtroom.

Eyebrows were raised in the courtroom when Morelli testified that it was her intention to have Joey Aulisio live at the residential ministry is Scranton—a released Joey Aulisio would be living within miles of Old Forge.

The mystery of the man sitting next to me in the courtroom with large art portfolio was solved when William Hinton was called to the witness stand on behalf of Joey Aulisio. There was nothing friendly toward me in the demeanor of Hinton. He brushed past me with the portfolio. He went by as though angry that I had dared testify against Joey.

For reference in his testimony, Hinton brought out from the portfolio twelve paintings by Joey Aulisio, including a painting of a mining village. I wondered, sitting in the courtroom, whether this painting represented the Connell's Patch neighborhood where Joey had lived. Some of the paintings were signed "AMD" ("after Mom died").

Mark Powell limited his cross-examination of Hinton, asking if the good professor had ever, in all his correspondence with Joey Aulisio since 2007, heard any expression of remorse for the murders. "No, sir," was the answer from Hinton. Behind me someone muttered, "You have to admit he's a good artist," to which someone else whispered in answer, "So was Hitler."

Joey Aulisio was finally called to the witness stand. All those present in the courtroom struggled to hear what Aulisio had to say as he spoke in a barely audible voice.

D'Andrea asked, "Let's go to July 26th, 1981. What could you tell us about that day?" Joey Aulisio's almost cavalier answer was stunning. "Well, that's the date Cheryl and Christopher died." D'Andrea asked Joey to recall the events of the day, and the world finally heard Aulisio's version of the crime: "Well, it seemed like a normal day, you know. I believe it was a Sunday. And, you know, I got up, you know, nothing seemed out of ordinary. I had no really plans to do anything or accomplish anything....But my older brother, he invited me to a softball game later on in the day. Later on that day, we went to the softball game. And I was there for maybe, you know, half an hour. And I don't really care for sports too much. So, I asked him to give me a ride back home. And he gave me a ride back home. And he dropped me off in front of the trailer."

D'Andrea continued his questioning. "So he dropped you off in front of your trailer?" "Yeah, he drops me off in front of the trailer, and Cheryl and Christopher come running over because they were in the next lot playing on the—it's like a big concrete pad that a trailer sits on. They come over. We were talking, you know and then, you know—the weather, it started—it was drizzling a little bit....It started to drizzle. So, we decided to, you know, go indoors. So, we walked across like 50 feet diagonal across the yard. We ended up in front of the house."

Joey Aulisio next testified that he had played with the Ziemba children previously in the new house. Aulisio explained that in the new house, since it was empty, they could get good "acoustics" while the children would go "hooting and hollering" while "almost like playing tag."

Joey Aulisio finally described the murders of Cheryl and Christopher Ziemba:

> *They were going from room to room running around.*
>
> *I think it was to the left, went into the bathroom. The acoustics were better in there. So I was, you know, I made some noise. And I was walking on my way out. And there was a closet there. I looked in the closet and there was a gun leaning up against the wall. And I looked at the floor right next to it. And there was a shell. So, I thought, you know, somebody put it there.*
>
> *And I thought that somebody took the shell out of it and put it on the floor right next to it indicating that it was empty you know. I come out of the bathroom.*
>
> *I took the gun. I picked it up. And I thought it was empty. I walked into—I think it was the master bedroom. So I walked in, right, and Cheryl was in there.*
>
> *And she was, you know, jumping around hollering. So I got the gun, you know, I said, "All right cops and robbers." I said stick 'em up right? So she stuck up her hands up. And the next thing I knew my ears were ringing. You know, the gun—it went off.*
>
> *I seen it go—you know, she got hit in the forehead. You know, I couldn't believe it. I just, you know, was shocked. I couldn't believe it. The only thing going through my head is, you know, what just happened. I couldn't believe it, you know.*
>
> *It was a—it was just a shock, you know. I couldn't believe it. I was like numb, you know. I couldn't comprehend what happened, you know.*
>
> *Well, after the gun went off, you know. I don't even remember reloading it, you know. I don't remember that. And he come running in. And I couldn't think, you know, what was going on. And I just panicked, you know, and shot him.*

Powell realized that Aulisio had just lied multiple times in his testimony. Cheryl had not been shot in the forehead—she had been shot in the back of her head while crouching down hiding in a closet rather than standing up.

Aulisio's testimony appeared contrived, mixing a little fact with a spinning of the evidence to put himself in the best light for the court.

Aulisio testified about what it was like to be sentenced to die in the electric chair: "That was another thing that was hard to believe, you know. It was just, you know, I remember when I was actually on death row, I would wake up every morning and I'd look at the door and say, Man, am I really here?"

Mark Powell pounced on cross-examination, peppering Aulisio with questions about the lies that he told in July 1981. Powell questioned Joey specifically about his sitting on the porch of the Ziemba home on the night of July 26, 1981, and how he watched Diane Ziemba cry. Aulisio stood by a few unsatisfying, almost rehearsed stock answers to Powell's questioning: "Counselor, that was a long time ago. I was in denial.…I don't remember too much.…I have a fragmented memory of 40 years ago."

Mark Powell dug at Joey, further asking, "After you blow Cheryl's brains out, you now get that gun, put another shell in to fire?" Aulisio meekly answered, "I told you I didn't recall that."

Powell twice asked the question, "You never told anyone where the murder weapon was?" Twice Joey Aulisio gave a nonanswer: "I pled not guilty and went to trial."

Joey Aulisio's cross-examination was not going well, and D'Andrea knew it. He raised an objection to attempt to shield his client from the onslaught of questions about the cover-up of the murders. "Your Honor, I'm going to keep objecting. My client didn't have to tell anybody anything."

Judge Geroulo addressed the objection sharply: "I take it that part of the defense position is remorse. I think something like that would indicate remorse. I'm going to overrule it. Next question."

Powell again questioned Aulisio about the location of the murder weapon:

> Mark Powell: "You never told anyone where the murder weapon was?"
> Joey Aulisio: "Again, I plead not guilty and went to trial."
> Powell: "Cheryl was actually in the closet when she was killed; isn't that correct?"
> Aulisio: "Ballistics say it must be true."

Powell followed up by mocking Joey Aulisio's assertion that the gun accidentally went off and killed Cheryl. "This gun accidentally went off when she was cower[ing] in the closet?" Joey Aulisio avoided the question: "I don't remember."

Ending his questions, Mark Powell rested the Commonwealth's case, and Geroulo now gave Powell and D'Andrea ten minutes each for their closing statements. Powell immediately went to the heart of the case against Joey Aulisio, noting that Judge Walsh, when Joey's death sentence had been vacated in 1987, sentenced Aulisio to consecutive life terms because he had intentionally killed not one but two children. Powell noted, "There is no volume discount if you kill more than one." He continued:

For thirty-seven years inmate Aulisio lied about his involvement in those murders. He covered his tracks, he misrepresented things in Court. He searched for the bodies with ----- and stood on the porch of the grieving mom and dad. For him to come to this Court today and suggest that this is an accident is so disingenuous. It's insulting and he doesn't even get his story straight because he said he killed Cheryl first and not Christopher.

Despite all the evidence at trial showing Chris was killed first and Cheryl was hiding in the closet when he blew her brains out. The shots were at point blank range. The hole in Chris's heart is a small hole, not one would expect from a 12-gauge shotgun fired from a distance. The point blank directed at his heart and the wad of the shell was imbedded in his chest.

And similarly, Cheryl was at point blank range when he blew her head off. And the wad of that shotgun was embedded in her brain matter. And then he covered his tracks. He did—all of his actions show a lack of remorse, show irresponsibility, and show cover up for an intentional killing. He disposed of those bodies like trash. All the time they were searching for the bodies, and he was participating in the search.

And Mr. Aulisio continued on a path of fear and threat, threatening five individuals. That directed to Mr. Kincaid about Cape Fear was intentional and methodical. That is a dangerous, dangerous man.

Mark Powell then addressed the impact of the murders on the Ziemba family. Speaking of the victim witness statements read in court, Powell noted, "The lives that he impacted are beyond Chris and Cheryl. He destroyed a family. He rocked a town. He wreaked havoc on many and he continued to do it after he was in prison."

D'Andrea, as Jack Brier had done thirty-eight years before, tried his best to spin a yarn favorable to Joey Aulisio. D'Andrea pointed out, "What Mr. Powell said and pointed his finger, he pointed at him all day. He said that man killed those children. But he was so wrong. It is this boy that did it, this child who killed those children....He was facing death by a very zealous prosecutor who wanted to see a fifteen-year-old die."

D'Andrea then discussed Joey Aulisio's incarceration: "He's done thirty-eight and a half years of hell. He's had no dignity ever in his life. He lived a lonely existence. He has shown compassion through his paintings. Hundreds of paintings showed compassion to people."

Judge Geroulo now addressed Joey Aulisio directly, asking, "Is there anything you would like to say at this point?" In a very soft, almost inaudible voice, Joey stated, "I'm sorry, Your Honor. I apologize to the Ziemba family, my family, and the public sir."

Joey Aulisio sat down. Looking directly at Joey Aulisio, Judge Geroulo stated:

> *Looking at those two little bodies that were thrown in that strip mine like garbage after they had been murdered, there are just no words to adequately describe the horribleness of that particular crime.*
>
> *The impact of the victim's family, again, searching for words conveying the horror of the impact, very very difficult. A mother who after thirty-eight years is too weak to come into court.*
>
> *Mr. Ziemba's life ended early under tragic terms obviously drawn a straight line to what took place in this case.*
>
> *The testimony of Brian Kincaid, while very remote in time, nevertheless indicates a sinister state of mind even at a point in time and one that I don't think can be totally disregarded.*

Judge Geroulo touched on Aulisio's upbringing and his efforts of rehabilitation. Judge Geroulo weighed this against Aulisio's accepting responsibility for his crimes:

> *When directed by his attorney to the date of July 26, 1981, his reply was and I wrote down the quote at the time, "That's the date Cheryl and Christopher died." He didn't state that that's the day he killed Cheryl and Christopher.*
>
> *It's almost as if it was their fault. That's the date that Cheryl and Christopher died. Then his words "The gun went off." Not I pulled the trigger. The gun went off almost as if it were the gun's fault.*
>
> *It was, "The gun went off. Cheryl died and then Christopher died." They were not actors here. They were recipients. And the statements of remorse and pretentions toward rehabilitation I think conflict very clearly*

in the mind of the fact that if we consider fifteen and a half years old, considered he was young, considering the minds of juveniles are different; nonetheless, that doesn't offset the hardness of the heart and the callousness of pretending to search, sitting on a porch with the families while the entire town was looking for the children.

The sophistication of what took place in the clean-up, the disposal and just the explanation offered here in court today that the first was accidental. The fact that he never told his original lawyer, his original trial might have been totally different approach had he done so. But couple that with thirty-eight years of denial and even when sentenced here today, he didn't admit that was an accident, a mistake, something that shouldn't have happen.

Judge Geroulo then sentenced Joey: "Accordingly, it will be the sentence of this court that you, Mr. Aulisio, are ordered to be incarcerated for a minimum period of time which shall be thirty years to a maximum which shall be life. And that sentence will be imposed on each count. And they will be served consecutively. In arriving at the consecutive sentence, I focus on the fact that I don't see any true remorse here. And any remorse that was expressed, I see as manipulation." Joey Aulisio bowed his head, dejected. Everybody in the courtroom rose. Aulisio was led out of the courtroom, as he had been in 1982.

Also present in the courtroom was Ernie Preate. Members of the press started to surround Preate, interviewing him and asking his opinion of the hearing. I began to make my way out of the courtroom. District Attorney Mark Powell approached me, shook my hand and stated to me, "You should finish working on that book you were writing."

Aulisio appealed his sentence. The Pennsylvania Supreme Court upheld Judge Geroulo's consecutive thirty-year to life sentences. Joey Aulisio will not be eligible for parole until July 29, 2041, sixty years to the date of his arrest.

SOURCES

Aulisio, Joseph. Correspondence with the author, May 5, 1993.

Aulisio, Robert, Sr. Interview with the author, April 1989.

Brier, Jack, defense attorney at trial for Joseph Aulisio. Interview with the author, May 1989.

Commonwealth v. Aulisio. Pennsylvania Supreme Court decision, 514 PA 84, 522 A.2nd 1075 (1987).

Commonwealth v. Joseph Aulisio. September 18, 2019. Resentencing hearing transcript.

Fox 56. Various reports, 2019–present.

Genova, Nicholas, Pennsylvania state trooper. Interview with the author, July 1996.

Jordan, Major Michael, Pennsylvania State Police. Interview with the author, August 1990.

Preate, Ernest, Jr., former Lackawanna County District Attorney. Interview with the author, November 1989.

Preliminary Hearing of Joseph Aulisio, October 1981. Transcript.

Robins, William. "Death Sentence for Pennsylvania Boy Reflects County's Mood, Judge Says." *New York Times*, June 14, 1982, section D, page 10.

Scranton Times-Tribune. Various articles, July 27, 1981–present.

Trial of Joseph Aulisio, May 1982. Trial transcript.

Wilkes-Barre Times Leader. Various articles, July 27, 1981–present.

WNEP Scranton. Various reports, 1981–2024. PAhomepage.com.

Zoltewicz, Stanley, Frank Genell, Mike Nalevanko and Edward Orzlek, Old Forge firefighters. Interviews with the author, 1990.

ABOUT THE AUTHOR

Brian W. Kincaid is a trial attorney who, for the past thirty-five years, has tried criminal and civil cases before the courts in the state of New Jersey and the Commonwealth of Pennsylvania. Part of Kincaid's law practice is devoted to crime victims' rights. Kincaid has held elected office as a councilman in the Borough of Mount Arlington, New Jersey. He has also served as a Morris County New Jersey rail freight commissioner and as well as Morris County tax commissioner. Kincaid also serves as a volunteer firefighter in the communities of Mount Arlington and Roxbury, New Jersey. Kincaid served as a witness on behalf of the Commonwealth during the December 2019 resentencing hearing in the *Commonwealth of Pennsylvania v. Joseph Aulisio* in December 2019. *Murder in Old Forge, Pennsylvania: The Tragic Death of the Ziemba Children* is his first book.